HODIO

Tales of an American P.O.W.

Clarence Nixon Day
of the   U.S.S. Houston

ICS Books, Inc.
Merrillville, Indiana

HODIO

Published by:
ICS Books, Inc.
1000 E. 80th Place
Merrillville, IN. 46410

Distributed by:
Stackpole Books
Cameron and Kelker Streets
Harrisburg, PA 17105

Library of Congress Cataloging in Publication Data

Day, Clarence Nixon, 1922-
  Hodio : tales of an American P.O.W.

  1. Day, Clarence Nixon, 1922-   . 2. World War,
1939-1945--Personal narratives, American. 3. World
War, 1939-1945--Prisoners and prisons, Japanese .
4. Prisoners of war--East Asia--Biography. 5. Prisoners of war--United States--Biography. I. Title.
D805.E18D38 1984   940.54'72'52   84-9074
ISBN 0-934802-13-0

Dedication

This book is lovingly dedicated to my family and friends who, through the long, uncertain years, never despaired that I was other than alive and would one day return home.

Also to my wife and children who tolerated my uncertainties, while writing and reliving some of the hell of being a Prisoner of War.

It is also a tribute to fellow shipmates of the U.S.S. Houston (CA-30) and the 2nd Battalion 131st Field Artillery, now known as the "Lost Battalion Association" of Texas. Never in our great nation's history, did our fighting men suffer more and perform as gallantly. I thank God daily for their helping to make it possible to fight the emotional aftermath of being a prisoner of war, and the patriotic brotherhood developed among us. They are all true red, white and blue; may God bless them all.

Clarence N. Day

FOREWORD

These are the experiences of a 19 year old caught by war. Made a prisoner by the Japanese in March 1942, he survived ordeals beyond the imagination of anyone who has never been a Prisoner Of War. The horrible feeling of being captured by an invincible enemy, half a world away from the safety of home, seeps through the pages of this book. It is hard to imagine how a teenage American, from a small town in Indiana, could even hope to survive. Indeed this survival was accomplished on a daily, even hourly basis. Many friends fell by the wayside. Many activities would have to be engaged in that would best be forgot.

But surviving this horror is only the beginning for a P.O.W. The lucky ones do survive, frequently to find a nightmare of readjustment ahead of them. Good friends have been left behind, often killed under brutal circumstances — events witnessed by the P.O.W. and burned into the memory. In the case of Clarence Day, the survivors of the U.S.S. Houston were all presumed dead — their very existence unknown until their liberation from camps at the war's end. Home was not the same, it never would be. Some wives of friends had remarried, all had been mourned as dead.

Years have past since these events. While some memories may have dulled, others suppressed, many events are as clear as the day they occurred. Writing this book was a painful experience. It forced many terrible things back into focus. But by completing it Clarence Day has allowed us to relive a piece of forgotten history, to experience an unimaginable nightmare. Some of the place names and vernacular have been misspelled, but this book has been published as it has been remembered.

"Horyo", which sounded to American ears as "hodio", meant Prisoner Of War. For the entire length of a very long war, this was the only title by which these young men were called. They came to identify themselves as miserable slaves, later as cleaver ruthless survivors— but always as "hodio."

About the Author

Clarence Nixon Day was born June 3, 1922, at North Terre Haute, Indiana, the son of Henry Howard Day and Lucy Day. His early years were spent on the streets of the city of Terre Haute, Indiana. He was graduated from Indiana State Laboratory School in the spring of 1940. Immediately joined the U.S. Navy and was assigned aboard the U.S.S. Houston and joined the Asiatic fleet until her famous sinking on February 28, 1942. He was captured on the island of Java and held prisoner for 42 months until his escape from Saigon, French Indo-China.

He returned to enter school at Indiana State University in June 1946, and was graduated in June 1949, with a B.S. degree in Physical Education and Industrial Arts. Since that time he has taught school and coached in Illinois and Indiana.

He and wife Barbara now reside in Merrillville, Indiana. They have four children; Diana, Donna, David, and Donald.

"Nick" as commonly known to his friends received the following service award medals: American Area, Asiatic-Pacific (three stars), Phillipine Defense (one star), American Defense (one star), Two Purple Heart Medals, Good Conduct Medal, China Service Award, World War II Victory Medal.

He hopes to retire soon and devote the rest of his life to his family and friends and write "Hodio" II.

1

Under the Rising Sun

A gentle rapping at the door aroused me from my slumber, as the morning sun peeked through the crack in the drawn drapes, striking me in the eyes. The room was heavy with the smell of Oriental perfume and stale tobacco smoke, and on the table were the remains of what looked like the leftovers of an elaborate drinking party.

Surely this is another dream, I thought, as I banged the side of my head. That drone of planes can't be for real. Rushing to the window, I jerked back the drapes and looked out into the steam rising from the hot, damp, blacktop street below. It didn't seem a bit unusual that a large Japanese flag was flying from the hotel across the street; I wondered why.

"It's sure a typical Asiatic city," I mused as I watched the hurry and scurry of the rick-shaws and people below. But why was I living here in such luxury when there was so much suffering in the world?

"I must be imagining those planes," I said as I turned to take stock of my surroundings. "Nice bed, and soft too-got a canopy with netting. I always wondered if there were mosquitoes up this high. That's a beautiful teakwood chest of drawers against that wall, but how do I know it's teakwood? These clothes look tailored, where did I get them? I'll try them on-well what do you know, a white tropical suit, a short sleeved white sport shirt. That's funny, I'm wearing a G-string, no shorts. Maybe it really isn't me. I'll look in the mirror."

My God, I thought, I'd better quit talking to myself; people will think I'm crazy if they see me. Again I heard the gentle rapping at the door. Moving toward the door I said, "Who is it?"

"Friend," they replied, "open the door."

I removed the chain and turned the lock; as I did so, the knob turned and the door quietly opened. Into the room came a tall Frenchman, dressed in tropical civilian clothes.

"How do you feel?" he asked. "You look a lot better than you did when I brought you here."

"How should I feel, and what am I doing here? I don't even know where I am."

"Well, you are Nick Day of the U.S. Navy, a former prisoner of war of the Japanese. In case you don't know it, you are now an escaped prisoner. I have kept you here for your own protection. You are in the Palace of Saigon Hotel, and under that Jap flag across the street is the Japanese Headquarters."

"How long have I been here?"

"Only three days, but don't worry, there is nothing wrong with you; just a little drunk and doped to help you get some rest and gain back your strength. The doctor gave you your last shot last night so you'll be alright now. I'll order you some food."

Walking over to the chest of drawers, he picked up the French style phone and ordered food to be sent to my room. Turning again to me he said, "You have nothing to worry about now; we will protect you until we can get you to your own people. So now, son, you take a nice bath, and by the time you finish, your food will be here. You eat and take a nice rest. I'll be back either this evening or tomorrow morning to see how you are getting along. If there is anything you need before I return, just pick up that phone and ask. Here're some smokes for you. Just don't open the door for anyone unless they knock softly three times just like I did." With this he got up, shook hands, said goodbye, and left.

"I wonder who he is-seems nice enough to me, but it sure is funny. Well, the man said to take a bath, so take a bath I will." The bath was all tile with shower and tub. "This is for me," I thought as I turned on the shower. "I wonder how long it's been since I've had a real decent bath, especially with soap. This will really be a pleasure just to stand here in the spray and soak awhile. Man, this water feels like needles and pins hitting my skin." While I was rubbing myself with a Turkish towel, I heard three soft knocks at the door.

"Just a minute," I said. Wrapping the towel around me, I opened the door to be greeted by a Chinese house boy with a cart full of food. He just grinned, pushed the cart inside, and left. The aroma from the food smelled so good I couldn't wait to dress and eat. Instead I just sat down on the bed, pulled the cart over, and ate my fill of hot steaming rice, seared meat, and some kind of root vegetables.

"Boy," I thought, "do I feel full. I think I'll just smoke a cigarette and lie back on the bed and relax a little while. I can't understand why the cleanliness, the odor and the softness of this bed seems to caress me so." Was I asleep, daydreaming, or was this just wishful thinking? How did I get into this situation? I believe I remember.

It all began on the fateful night of February 21, 1942, in beautiful Sunda Straits, between the island of Java and Sumatra. I was wearing a pair of earphones, laying on the deck of the U.S.S. Houston, but being weary from battles we'd recently fought, I dozed off. I hadn't been asleep long when I received the following message:

"We expect to engage a small enemy task force within the next few hours. Be alert for such a force." I casually leaned back and rested, thinking nothing more of the situation. Before the next few hours elapsed, I intended to be caught up on sleep.

The resounding boom of guns told me in no uncertain terms what I could do with my intentions! I rushed to my battle station, with my energy somehow suddenly restored. It seemed that we were being fired upon from all directions. The Australian light cruiser **Perth,** steaming ahead of us, was already listing badly and obviously was about to sink. Seeing her in this condition, I finally realized what was going on.

We were right in the middle of a Japanese landing-force convoy. No one seemed to know the actual number of Japanese ships, but we were surrounded. As they closed in on us, some of our crew were standing on deck firing small arms and throwing debris onto the decks of the enemy ships.

"Torpedos on the starboard side!" someone screamed, and I hit the deck. With each hit, the ship rocked and bucked like a bronco. I counted them as I clawed at the cold steel deck: one-two-three-four! My God, I thought, how much can she take? The starburst of an exploding shell illuminated the flag on her aft flagstaff in a final burst of glory; then, during a sudden lull in the battle, she began quietly and majestically to slide beneath the water.

"Now hear this, now hear this, all hands abandon ships, all hands abandon ship!" Amazed and still only half believing what was happening, I saw the bugler standing on the wing of the flight deck like a statue, sounding the call to abandon ship.

I ran to the main deck aft, sat down alongside the number three turret, took off my shoes and socks, got up and took a farewell look about, climbed up through the life-line, walked down her side to the screw guard, and plunged into the sea.

When I hit the water, it felt as if someone had hit me in the face with a wet oily rag. The life jacket I had on seemed to tear at my shoulders as I shot up to the surface.

"Oh God," I prayed, "what do you do in a situation like this? Here I'm awakened from my sleep and suddenly find myself in the middle of the sea, floating debris, oil and flames, amid hundreds of screaming, wounded, helpless people."

My prayers must have been answered because I suddenly realized that I was very calm, considering the circumstances; so I began trying to take stock of the situation. Thanking God that I could swim sufficiently well to do so, I set about helping gather up the seriously wounded and getting them into life rafts, where they might have a possible chance of survival.

Among those in the water whom I contacted at this time was our chaplain from aboard ship. He was Commander Rentz, an elderly and fatherly type gentleman whom I had always loved and respected. He could not swim.

"I'm just a burden to you men," he said, "just let me over the side, and it will be easier for you to navigate this life raft against the tide." I helped put him safely aboard the life raft and tried to convince him how necessary and helpful his presence was to us in our time of trial. Everyone on the raft and ropes with me just ignored his request and went ahead pushing and pulling, trying to navigate the non-swimmers and wounded toward shore.

"Please," he said, "just let me get on the back of the raft and kick my feet; maybe my efforts can help in a small way to propel the raft through the water." After hours of pushing, pulling and swimming to ease his anxiety, we finally let him get outside the raft, and hanging on the back, kick his feet to help propel the raft.

The next thing I knew he had let loose, removed his life jacket, and was saying a prayer, for us, as he vanished under the waves and sank from sight. His sacrifice began to make me realize more than ever the seriousness of my situation. I started to think and wonder-is it a hopeless task when a man of that caliber could give his life so easily, in the hope of giving us a better chance for survival?

Here I was, only eighteen years of age, thrown into a situation like this. Ahead of me, at a distance, I could see land on the horizon. How far it was I didn't know. Approximately ten to fifteen miles, I guessed, but the tides in the strait were so swift and changed directions so often, it was almost impossible to make any headway against them.

So, looking up into the heavens, I prayed to God, "As long as You, Dear God, give me the life in my body, I will fight to preserve it, no matter what comes."

During the course of that night, as I struggled to survive, I had many uncanny experiences which couldn't be accounted for or explained in terms of any ordinary frame of reference. I have always contended that one of these, in particular, saved my life. It happened during the early morning hours, just before sunrise. After being in the salt water all night, I was very hungry and thirsty. I suddenly came upon a wooden potato crate floating on the surface, Upon examining it, I discovered it contained a small, rotten onion and one shriveled, dried-up potato. These two rotten vegetables, which a few short hours ago would have been repulsive, were now the staff of life to me, and I heartily devoured them.

The sun came up over some mountains which must have been on the island of Java. Its warmth would have felt good on my face if it hadn't been for the glare on the water. Squinting in an effort to screen out the glare, I spotted a boat coming toward me. Oh, no! It couldn't be! Feeling a sudden rush of adrenalin, I prepared to take a dive, just in case the boat's crew should decide to open up on me with that maching gun mounted on the front. They slowed down alongside me. Shading my eyes with my hand, I looked up into the grinning animal-like face of a Japanese Marine. He reached down, grabbed me by the wrist, and helped me into the boat. Jerking me up to a sitting position, he immediately tied my hands behind my back.

The boat banged to a stop alongside the gangway of a Jap ship and as I looked around, I discovered I was not the only one in the boat. They had picked up eight of us. Herding us up the gangway, they marched us astern, and lined us up in single file facing forward. I was on the extreme left end of the line, near the port side of the ship.

The Jap in charge barked out orders, and through the hatch in front of us came eight more Japs in complete uniform, carrying rifles and fixed bayonets. Someone alongside of me said, "My God, a firing squad!"

My thoughts began to race, In a flash I wondered if my life had come to an end. "No," I decided, "if they are going to shoot me, I'll either be going toward them or running away. I will not stand and die helplessly." Just as the firing squad were loading their guns and getting ready to shoot, a Jap officer came running from the hatch of the ship screaming, "Mati, Mati". At this time I had no idea what these words meant, but I didn't care because they had stopped the firing squad. I later learned they meant, "Wait, Wait!"

So rather than be responsible for our deaths, the cunning Japs loaded us back into the landing barge, took us back out to the middle of the Straits and threw us back into the waters from whence we had come. They must have felt sure we would drown and consequently they would not be directly responsible for our deaths.

2

Crossing Enemy Lines

Once again I started out swimming toward land on the distant horizon. By now my chances of making it were very poor, as I was hungry and exhausted, but I knew I would try as long as it was humanly possible. I swam until it seemed I couldn't raise my arms, then turned over on my back to float awhile. By alternately swimming and floating, I managed to keep going until late in the evening when I was suddenly picked up by a swift tide and thrown onto the beach on which the Japanese had already landed. Very cautiously crawling down the sands of the beach, I came to a native boat in which I took cover. When the native Javanese came back for his boat, I forced him to go back out into the straits, and I started picking up all the survivors I could find in the late dusk. Upon returning to the beach, we split up, and all started crawling over the sand, making our way to the underbrush. I hoped to get through the Jap lines and rejoin the Allied Forces.

All up and down the coastal roads of the beach, the Japanese had sentries posted within calling distance of each other, so getting through the lines presented quite a problem. Crawling cautiously over to a coconut tree, under cover of some banana leaves, I laid quietly and listened. To my startled surprise, there was a Jap sentry on the other side of the tree, standing at parade rest with his rifle between his feet as if he were half-asleep.

"Oh God," I prayed, "please give me strength." Moving quietly, I grabbed him from behind by the throat and as he slumped to the ground I caved his head in against the side of the tree. "It seemed so easy, so unreal," I thought. "He didn't even struggle much." Can I ever forget the feeling and sound of those dying gurgles under my hands?

I dashed across the road and into the jungle, crawling and running on and on until I was completely exhausted and either passed out or fell asleep.

Upon awakening in the morning, I had a feeling of loneliness and fear I had never had before, so I started off once more through the jungle, having no idea of either time or direction. Two or three hours later I heard voices. It can't be, I thought.

"Hey! you guys," I called. "Where are you?" Everything got quiet; I guess they thought I was a Jap trying to trick them. No one answered, so I plodded on through the jungle a short way. Then I heard someone say, "There he is! Hey, Day! We are over here - come to your right!"

Changing direction and heading to my right, I came to a clearing where there were nine disheveled, wounded, partially clothed starving shipmates, who had also gotten through the lines of the Japs as I had. Command of our crew was immediately assumed by Lieutenant J.G. Hamlin, a short stocky fellow from the steel mills of Kokomo, Indiana, who had his training at Annapolis and was well versed in the ways of the Orient. We sat down and laid plans. We would try to make our way to the town of Tilichap on the opposite side of Java where we knew there were American ships and subs. From there we might be able to reach safety.

We started out in single file, following paths, roads and even railways, in the general direction of Tilichap. When we reached the foothills of the mountains, we discovered the thick undergrowth was much better protection than we had hoped for in our efforts to avoid detection by the Japs.

Walking quietly along the edge of a grove of trees, I was startled by a loud screech close by. Right across my path ran a screaming monkey, being chased by a gorgeous black panther. The sun glistened on the panther's beautiful black coat as it ran with the ease and grace of a ballet dancer. This wild beast in his natural habitat was an unforgettable sight.

When darkness came on, I was again exhausted. Covering myself with jungle leaves, I spent another anxious night. Upon awakening, I found my hunger and thirst were serious problems, which had to be solved if I were going to survive. The only food I knew of in the jungle was the coconuts, and the meat and milk from these had so far sustained me. With no weapons, it was impossible to kill game for food. I also realized that we needed weapons for protection from the Japs, natives, and wild beasts alike. Most of us were partially dressed, as in the tropics a minimum of clothing is worn because of the intense heat. My skin was peeling off because of the oil and gasoline in the water when our ship went down, and my feet were sore and blistered from walking over the hot jungle paths. I woke up to the fact that war was hell and that I would probably have to kill and steal for things that were necessary for my survival.

With such thought dominating our minds, we continued on our way until we came upon a small native village where we were approached by a Chinaman who spoke English. He told us he was a storekeeper and the natives from the surrounding areas were about to raid the village. It had already been evacuated by the townspeople, who had locked up their homes and stores and left. He said if we would protect him from the natives while he gathered up his personal belongings, we would be welcome to anything in his store. Realizing our need for food and weapons, we agreed to go with him.

Upon reaching the end of the main street of this village I saw what seemed to me like hundreds of natives milling about, a yelling, screaming, ferocious mob. They would converge upon a store, smash their way through windows and doors, and proceed to strip the stores of everything they wanted.

Unnoticed, we circled around behind them and entered the Chinaman's store. While he gathered his belongings, we grabbed whatever food and weapons we thought would help us. Unfortunately, the looting natives also had their eyes on the shop and we soon found ourselves surrounded.

Lt. Hamlin yelled orders for us to form a tight single-file line, with each of us grabbing the man in front of him in a bear hug. In this fashion, he'd try to lead us through the mob. He told us not to assault any native unless they started something.

We began to inch our way slowly through the mass of natives. Bringing up the rear was our short, fat Chief Bandmaster, whom we'd nicknamed "Bandy." He'd scrounged a meat cleaver from the Chinaman's store, and was brandishing it in one hand while hanging onto the man in front of him with the other.

Suddenly our line halted. The men in the rear shoved as hard as they could, trying to force us through. After what seemed like an eternity, we began to move again. We broke into the open and ran for our lives.

We made our way to the Chinaman's house on the edge of the village. Realizing that the natives had not pursued us, we stopped to take inventory. It was then that we learned why our line had stopped in the midst of the mob. One of the natives had spotted Lt. Hamlin's Annapolis class ring, and had robbed him of it. Unknowingly, the pushy-shovey guys at the rear of the line had been forcing the Lieutenant's gut toward the blade of a bolo knife!

At first we were all mad as hell over the robbery, and we recklessly vowed we would go back and recover the ring. But good sense prevailed; we soon realized the hopelessness of the task, and decided to go on.

The rewards of our effort had been few. Our inventory showed a hammer, a meat cleaver, one butcher knife, a little salt, a few pieces of cloth and a sack of hard candy. Thanking us and wishing us luck, the Chinaman departed, and we proceeded down a railway through the jungle in what we thought was the direction of Tilichap. This was a very mountainous country and we soon discovered it would be impossible to continue down the railway. The bridges had all been blown up and Jap planes were patrolling it continuously, so we again took to the jungle paths.

As we stumbled wearily on, time and time we came upon a group of natives fleeing before the Jap army, as we were. From these natives we learned there was a village still occupied by the Dutch, in the near vicinity. My hopes rose immediately, and my pace quickened when I realized that maybe with luck, we might have a possible chance to get out of here. About thirty-six hours later we came struggling into the village and made our way to the village square.

Across the street came a high-ranking Dutch army official, in a green suit and gold braid.

"You men just take it easy," Lt. Hamlin said, "I'll do the talking for us." Approaching the Dutch officer, he extended his hand and said Hello."

"Yah," the Dutchman said, "I am acting Dutch Resident of this town, I have been told by the native drums of your coming arrival. I'll put you up for the night and provide, you all with some food and clothing. Please follow me." He led us around the square, through a gate of stone fence and compound to a native hospital.

"You take your men in here and rest. I'll return in a little while with food for you." As he left, we entered the door and found that the building consisted of three large rooms, connected by archways. Inside were four teakwood beds with rope webbing to sleep on. Being utterly exhausted, we all found a place to lie down and rest.

In what seemed like a very short time, the Dutchman returned with several servants. They were carrying halves of coconut shells filled with steaming rice, with a half of a boiled egg on top of each.

"I'm sorry I can't get you any more food than this, but with a couple cups of hot tea, maybe it will tide you over until we do better. We'll leave here the first thing in the morning. You men get a good night's sleep and I'll have a truck waiting for you in the morning to take you to the Allied Forces."

"Just a minute, sir," Lt. Hamlin said. "I understand the Japs are paying bounties to the natives to kill us or turn us over to them. Therefore I feel we must have some guns or weapons of some kind to protect ourselves from them."

"I'll see what I can do for you. I know I can at least get you a few pistols, but I must go now. Lock yourselves in, and you'll be safe until I return." With this he took hurried leave of us. Feeling very contented after our meager rations, we barred all the doors and windows and settled down for the night.

Upon arising the next morning, as the sun came up, I found I could hardly breathe the rank, musty air inside the closed and barred building. So, seeking some fresh air, I walked out into the compound. I was horrified to find our Dutch friend's mutilated body, scattered about, and hundreds of natives milling around outside the compound. I ran back inside to arouse the others, but was so scared I couldn't get the words out. Finally, Lt. Hamlin got me calmed down enough to find out what was wrong.

"O.K. men," he ordered, "get together, grab anything you want of any value and let's get the hell out of here!"

By banding together and walking steadfastly through them while brandishing our knife, meat cleaver and hammer, we made our escape. They seemed afraid to attack us as long as we were in a group. We moved quickly as possible away from that area, fearing pursuit from both the natives and the Japs. We headed in a northeasterly direction, going up a blacktop road. The retreating Allied Forces had blown bridges and felled trees across the road; it was like an obstacle course. I breathed a sigh of relief as we moved over the top of the mountain, traveling in single file. I was the last man in line, and the others had all passed the small hut by the side of the road before a small dark-skinned girl emerged. She appeared to be about five years old. She walked up to me, took hold of my hand and said, "Where are you going?" in perfect English.

"I do not know, my dear," I said, "but we are trying to get to Tilichap."

"Oh," she replied, "but you are going in the wrong direction. You must go back or the natives will kill you."

I immediately called a halt and told Lt. Hamlin of my encounter. It was hard for him to believe, as it was for me, that the little girl spoke fluent English. Upon questioning her, we found that her father had been an English seaman and her mother the daughter of a native tribal chieftan. She had lived the life of a white girl and had been schooled by English missionaries. She was still holding my hand as she led us back in the opposite direction to a grove of rubber trees. She stopped, turned to the natives who had been following us, and screamed at them in their own dialect. They just seemed to fade away.

"Now," she said, "go through these trees until you reach the road like the one you have been on, and follow it to your left. Goodbye, and good luck. I hope someday we meet again. " She turned and headed back toward her home as we stared at her in unbelieving wonder.

We proceeded hastily until we came to the road and turned down it. Then our pace slackened and we followed the road for several hours before we reached the higher peaks of the mountains. I began to realize why our progress was so slow. Our bodies were swollen from insect bites, our skin was peeling, and our feet were blistered from traveling on the hot roads. Due to the condition of some of the fellows, we picked the first secluded clearing as a place to sleep for the night. We all lay huddled against each other on the moist ground, hoping the body heat from each other might keep us warm.

It seemed like I had just gone to sleep when suddenly I had an eerie feeling something was wrong. Struggling with my swollen eyelids, I looked up and around into a sea of native faces, grinning and bearing down on us. I woke the guy next to me and he woke the guy on the other side of him, setting off a chain reaction. We lay quietly at first, discussing what to do. Then I suggested, "Let's all jump at once and give the proverbial Indian war whoop and see if we can frighten them away."

"Sounds like a good idea," Lt. Hamlin answered, "let's try it on the count of three. One----two----three!" We jumped to our feet and began to yell like a bunch of Comanches, and the natives fled. We grabbed two or three stragglers and forced them to climb coconut trees for us, so we could again have some nourishment.

After finishing our meal of green coconut meat and milk, we started off again, and after a few hours we were approached by a native in a black sarong, and wearing a white shirt. He spoke English and said, "I will be glad to lead you to the Dutch forces."

So, being gullible, we agreed to follow him. After some time, it suddenly dawned on us that we were going down out of the mountains. Upon questioning our guide, his story was that we must go to this certain village in the foothills of the mountains to join the Dutch forces. Coming to a crossroads, he told us he must leave us and showed us the road to take. We thought he had done us a great favor, so thanking him profusely, we continued on alone.

Coming down through a beautiful valley, with fields of rice on each side of the road, we spotted flags flying in the distant haze up ahead, which we believed were Red Cross flags. So, rejoicing thankfully, we quickened our pace. We came to a small bridge across a drainage ditch of some kind, with a meadow-like stream of water running under it. As we crossed it and climbed a very sharp hill on the other side, we were horrified to find ourselves looking into the barrels of two Jap machine guns. We immediately retreated back down the hill and dove into the ditch for cover. The betrayal be our friend who had led us from the mountain was now evident.

Lt. Hamlin crawled very cautiously to the center of the road behind the hill and motioned for us to join him. We were a disheveled mess by this time for our ten days in the jungle had been very tiring; most of us were at a loss for what to do or what to say or how to act. We were so starved and exhausted that our thoughts were incoherent and our minds were numb.

We held a conference to decide what we were going to do, but arrived at no concrete decisions. Then one boy with us who was expended to about the limit of human endurance said, "I'll go up and see what the Japs have to say." Before we had a chance to do anything about it, he got up, put his hands above his head and quietly went up over the hill to face the Japanese.

I gasped, "What do you think of that? He either must be awful brave or nuts."

I crawled to the break of the hill and could see the Japs talking to him. Then he turned and came back towards us as if he didn't have a worry in the world. He seemed to breathe a sigh of relief as he related his message.

"There's a Jap officer up there who speaks English and says if we value our lives, we will all come up the road and be taken prisoners.

After some discussion, everyone decided to go except one redheaded fellow and myself.

After being in the Orient eighteen months, I had heard stories of the beheading of the Chinese and other atrocities of the Japs and I decided I would just as soon be dead as be taken prisoner by the Japs and be tortured and killed. Therefore, when the other eight men went up the road to be taken prisoners, Red and I started to run down a small drainage ditch. Suddenly there was a deafening roar of gunfire and I hit the filthy mud, water and slime in the bottom of the grass-covered drainage ditch.

It got deathly quiet, and as I slowly looked up from the

water in the bottom of the drainage ditch, I looked into the barrels of their guns. They looked as big as cannons. I heard Red moan. Glancing back, I discovered he had been shot in the leg. They roused us to our feet with bayonets and proceded to march us up the road to our companions. In the middle of a crossboard, a small, high ranking Jap officer stood waiting our arrival. He looked at me, grinned and said, "Son, either you are very brave or you are crazy, one or the other."

3

The Gates of Hell

I was surprised to find that these Japanese Marines who had captured me were strong, healthy men -- big in stature, and mentally and physically alert. They seemed to respect the position we were in, and treated us with the consideration due a fellow fighting man. This was in drastic contrast to the treatment I later encountered from the ordinary prisoner of war guards. Cold chills ran up my spine as they searched me, tied my wrists together behind my back so tightly they hurt, and fastened me to the rope which held my shipmates. Turning us toward the village, they marched us down the middle of the road, which was lined on each side with jeering natives waving small Jap flags.

"Tang Juan Priok! What a heck of a name for a town," I said. "Typical of small Oriental towns, it's beautiful, though; only it's a shame we can't enjoy it."

Marching us through the gate of a high stone wall which

surrounded a small native prison, they stopped us in a cobblestone compound. My hands were untied and I was led by a Jap on each side and thrown into a small, dark, damp cell. As the door clanged shut we were all picking ourselves up when Lt. Hamlin said, "Well, the Gates of Hell just closed, men. We are now prisoners of war!"

My fate, I knew now, was entirely in the hands of the Japanese. Where I went from here, or what they might do with me, I did not know. So, as others sobbed, I gave a 'what the hell' sigh and immediately laid down to stretch my weary aching bones and muscles.

After a while, my shipmates and I were thrown into a Japanese truck that was strictly a replica of the American U.S. Army Chevrolet truck. They called it a "Neisan." After being loaded into this convoy of trucks, I began to feel the Japanese were much more afraid of us than we were of them. On top of each truck cab they had a machine gun pointing into the bed of the truck on us, and sitting up on each of the four corners of the truck bed there was a guard with a rifle and fixed bayonet, plus hand grenades, to see that we made no attempt to escape. In this fashion, we started down the beautiful mountain valley roads of Java, lined with lush green fields and heavy vegetation, which eventually broadened into a low, sweeping valley with but one large lonely looking tree. The convoy stopped and the guards began a discussion, pointing to the tree. I believed my end had come. Had they brought us here for the purpose of executing us under this tree?

Suddenly, from the opposite direction, a Japanese command car approached with fully military escort. They stopped and an officer got out and came over to peer into the truck at us. Our guards kicked us to our feet so we could be viewed like monkeys in a zoo. He stood and talked to his fellow officers, touching and poking fun at us, as if to gloat in the glory of their victory.

The Japanese officer who was standing within five feet of where I was standing in the truck, pulled out a package of cigarettes and started to light one. When he did so, I reached out and made a motion to indicate I would like one too. Immediately a rifle butt crashed into my skull and sent me reeling to the bottom of the truck. As I staggered back to my feet, the Japs all laughed at me as though it was a big joke. The Jap officer made motions to me, as if inquiring what I wanted, and with sign language I indicated all I wanted was a cigarette. When he understood what I wanted, he threw me his whole pack of cigarettes, then turned around, barking orders at his staff officers. They in turn called up a Jap sotjo, which is the equivalent of our staff sergeant who proceeded to get all the cigarettes and rations his troops had and threw them in to us. The rations were our major concern, and we devoured them like wolves.

A couple of native women came down the road selling baskets of bananas and other tropical fruits. Realizing the extent of our hunger, the officer (or the sotjo???) also confiscated these and threw them in to us. I didn't quite understand the meaning of why they were doing such a thing for us, but later I realized that they were the Japanese front line troops and they were more or less doing this as a gesture of mutual respect.

After things had calmed down a little and we had eaten and felt better with a full stomach, the Japanese officer told the Sergeant in charge of our trucks to take us to a town called Serang Java. So, with all honors due an officer, and after much bowing, saluting, and scraping as he departed, our drivers climbed back into the trucks, started the engines, and we once more started down through the tropical valleys typical of this end of Java.

After another three or four hours of riding in the dust and hot tropical sun, we arrived at Serang. Upon reaching this town, we started down a beautiful boulevard, past a Dutch resident's home, up a hill, and halted in front of the Jap headquarters. We were unloaded from the trucks, and tying our hands and feet securely, they set us on the lawn to wait with a few soldiers as guards to see that we made no attempt to untie ourselves and escape. After we had set in this cramped position for some time, darkness approached and it began to rain. Still no movement of any kind was made to do anything with us. Finally, after what seemed an endless time, a Jap came out on the veranda of their headquarters, barked commands to the guards in charge of us, and, kicking us to our feet, told us we were to be interrogated.

A table was brought out on the veranda and an interpreter came out and seated himself at it. One by one we were brought before him to be questioned. When my turn came, I was seated on a box across from the Jap interpreter and the first thing he said was,

"Nam-o?"

I told him my name was C.N. Day. It was hard for a Jap to understand that anyone would have a name spelled just D-A-Y. He thought it was impossible that Day was the only name I had, and therefore concluded that I was lying to him. According to the Japanese military tradition, there is nothing worse than a liar, so they immediately began to beat me around. They questioned everyone else, satisfied their whims, put them back out on the lawn in the rain, and turned to me again.

Again he asked my name and again I said, "C.N. Day." They just couldn't believe anyone could have a name like mine. After continually beating and questioning me, they finally called in another interpreter, who in turn sat down across from me and asked,

"What is your name?"

I wearily replied, "My name is C.N. Day."

"Oh! Osaka," he said, "Conday."

Rather than go through another beating I said, "Yes, my name is Conday."

Conday was perfectly satisfying to the Japs, because to them it sounded like a Japanese name. So, for the next forty-two months as a prisoner of war, I was officially listed on the Jap records as Conday. I wondered whatever happened to just plain old Nick Day.

After this interrogation, we were marched across the street, around the side of a house, to a one-car garage. There they sat us down in the driveway in the rain and proceeded to have an elaborate discussion as to what they were going to do with us. Finally, after what seemed like endless misery, they decided to take us into the garage to spend the night. One by one, they took us into the garage and squatted us down on our feet and legs in this confined area, where we could move in no direction because of being tied together. It was here, amid fear and worried thoughts that I spent my first night as a prisoner of war.

4

The Horrors of War

Early the next morning they came and got us. I'll never forget the pain I endured as I tried to stand. Somehow I managed to hobble down the street under the guard's rifles and bayonets. They brought us to an abrupt halt in front of a beautiful Dutch home that was elaborately furnished with teakwood desks, leather upholstered chairs, sofa, and luxurious carpeting. It was there that I really began to see the horrors of war.

There were signs everywhere of frantic evacuation as this family had been forced to flee their lovely home. On the table was a photograph album where several pictures had been hastily torn out. As I looked it over, I couldn't help but wonder about this family. The refrigerator door stood open and there were pieces of clothing that had been dropped in haste throughout the house.

The Jap sergeant put us to work helping carry all of the furniture outdoors where we stacked it in one huge pile.

Just as I threw the last rug on top, a Jap guard emptied the contents of a gasoline can over the pile and set a match to it. We were then taken to the Jap Quartermaster depot where we got grass mats. We returned to the empty house with the mats and installed them for the Japs to sleep on. The house was to be living quarters for the officers in charge of our imprisonment. The contrast between the meager furnishings the Japs preferred and the lovely furniture we had destroyed led me to conclude that the Japanese had never been taught to appreciate the finer things of life and in many ways were like savages.

We repeated this process at several homes during the morning. When they finally decided they were through with us, they loaded us into trucks and hauled us to the Serang Prison. As our truck came to a halt outside the prison, the smell of the filth, and staleness on the inside was evident. The outside wall of stucco was about ten feet high, and broken glass and sharp spikes covered the top. High iron gates filled the arch where we were supposed to enter. The gates were opened for us by sneering criminal-looking natives, backed up by Japs with rifles and fixed bayonets. As I marched through the arch and the gates clanged behind, I looked over to a buddy marching beside me and said, "Well, I guess the gates of Hell have just closed on us." Little did I know how much truth there was in those words.

We entered a compound which had cobblestone flooring, with an old pulley-type well in the center. Cells surrounded the compound. Prison guards began to grab us, one at a time, kicking and shoving us into cells. I landed on the cold stinking concrete floor of the cell. As I was being helped to my feet I heard shouts of welcome. After my head cleared and I got my bearings, I began to recognize those around me as fellow shipmates who had ended up here, as I had.

A little while later, after they had quieted down, I made the remark that it was awfully crowded in here. Someone spoke up and said, "Hell, you ain't seen nothing yet."

My cell was about fourteen by twenty-eight feet with one small window up at the back and one small door just four feet by six. It also had slanted concrete slabs on each side, forming an aisle down the middle. Considering there were seventy-four of us in here, we didn't have much room. It was impossible for everyone to sit or lay down at the same time, so we had to stand up or sleep in shifts.

My days and nights were endless in this prison cell. Food and water seemed to be practically unheard of, as far as the Japs were concerned. My food here consisted of one ball of gummy rice per day and a small can of boiled water, still warm, about every third day. Toilet facilities consisted of a half of a wooden barrel standing in one corner, which was soon running over. It was no wonder, after the first few days, everyone began getting sick.

The cell to the right of us, housed eighty women of all ages, and nationalities, plus a large number of children, who were not counted by the Japs in filling up the cells. I don't think I'll ever forget the sorrow I felt for those women and children crowded into a mass of human suffering.

On the morning of my tenth day in this cell, a Jap came into the compound with a piece of paper from which he began to read in Japanese. The first thing he read that I could understand was 'Conday,' so I called from the cell door. Our guards brought him over to my cell. He wanted to know if my name was Conday and I answered yes, so he ordered the guards to go get the turnkey, unlock the door and let me out in the compound. While I was waiting in suspense, I remarked to my buddies in the cell with me, "If any of you so and so's want to go in my place, speak up." Of course, everyone thought I was going to be tortured or shot, so no one volunteered to take my place.

After they got me out of the cell, the Jap handed me the paper from which he had been reading. It had ten names listed on it, the first of which was mine. Through sign language, he made me understand that he wanted me to call these names. The guards took me to the door of each cell where I read the list. One fellow was sick and unable to be removed from his cell, so the Jap in charge told me to pick out one more man. I was looking around for someone I knew when I heard a voice call,

"Hey, Mate, don't I know you?" Looking toward the door of the cell from where the call had come, I spotted this short, stocky, roly-poly Italian-looking fellow sitting in the sun behind the bars. I recognized him as a shipmate from the Houston, but didn't know his name, so I said,

"I don't know, but if you want out of that cell, say so. You're our boy."

"Hey, tell the yellow bastards to open the door," he replied.

I turned to the Jap and motioned for him to open the door, that this guy would go. After he got out of the cell, he introduced himself as Hank Barbetti. I knew right away that we would become fast friends.

They took us to the middle of the compound and lined us all up in one rank with guards all around. Out strutted a Jap officer, who climbed up on a box to give us a speech. In broken English he said, "Due to the fact that our Emperor has a kind heart, you have been taken prisoners of war. But, you must work, you must work hard, you must work with all your might and main!"

I laughed. There was a blinding flash; I saw stars and immediately found myself on the cobblestone floor. I'd been rapped by a Jap guard's rifle butt. I had learned a valuable and important lesson: never laugh at a Jap, especially if he had the upper hand, as his sense of humor differs so greatly from my own. After I struggled back to my feet and order was restored, he proceeded to tell us we were to work as a detail of trustees inside the prison.

We were taken to the front of the prison and put in a cell by ourselves, with the door unlocked and left open. Therefore we had the freedom to roam inside the prison walls. We were also told that they would supply us with shoes and clothing. After talking and getting better acquainted with my new cellmates, I came to realize that we were the youngest military prisoners the Japs had, in this prison at least, and decided they had picked us because we would probably be easier to handle than the older fellows.

As I was touring the prison, and more or less just visiting with the other prisoners, I was called to the door of a cell next to my old cell, the one filled with women. The Dutch lady who called me wanted to know if I could get medical help of some kind from the Japs. She said a young girl in the cell with them was having a baby. Excitedly I rushed back to the front of the prison and found the Jap sergeant in charge. I told him what was going on as best I could with the language barrier, and finally convinced him that the girl was in grave danger if he didn't get a doctor to her quickly. I also told him that a doctor from our ship was here in prison and that he would be glad to help her. I led him to the cell which housed Dr. Burroughs. After we'd gotten the doctor from the cell and explained to him what was going on, a Jap officer arrived on the scene and refused to let him enter the women's cell to help the girl. But in spite of the Japs, the mother and baby got along fine, and we had an increase in prison population.

5

Unrewarded Valor

While I was in Serang Prison, I met Mrs. Lowry, whose husband had been secretary of the Y.M.C.A. in Singapore. I was lounging around the compound one evening, and spotted her standing alongside the prison wall, waiting to be interrogated. I noticed that her eyes had that blank look one gets when suffering from shock or near death. Talking to me as if she were in a trance, she recounted the story of Margie.

It seemed that Margie had been quite a rounder before the war; a "B-girl" and nightclub entertainer in the Orient. When the war started, she had been working as a night nurse in the English hospital in Singapore and was trapped there.

During an air raid which preceded the invasion, she was hit by a piece of shrapnel which tore off about half of her left breast. She applied a pressure bandage and went right ahead serving those who were wounded worse than she,

—35—

until the Japs actually invaded the hospital, killing the patients in their beds.

To escape the onrushing Japanese, Margie left the hospital, made her way to the docks, and boarded a small inter-island steamer. There were about 48 civilians and a large number of children aboard. Two of the children, a boy five years of age, and a girl of eight, were in Mrs. Lowry's care. She and Margie met aboard the steamer, and quickly became fast friends.

On the second day out, pursuing Japanese planes bombed and strafed the ship. A direct hit on the open sea would have sunk her, drowning most of the children and creating mass hysteria. Realizing this, the captain chose to run aground off the coast of Sumatra. As the tiny vessel lay on the coral reef at the mercy of the attacking Japanese planes, Margie took charge and began to issue orders like a general. She supervised the evacuation of the wounded, then made ten or more trips back to the abandoned steamer for supplies. Her shuttle runs were finally halted by a direct hit which sent the ship sliding beneath the sea.

One of the survivors was wounded, burned, and suffering from shock and concussion. He screamed and begged for someone to help him or put him out of his misery. Margie, realizing that this outburst was devastating to the morale of the children, gently lifted him and carried him into the dense wooded area surrounding the beach. As soon as she was out of sight, she set him against a tree, picked up a club and proceeded to beat his brains out.

After getting the rest calmed down, she said she would take off, head south down the coast to the Allied Forces, and get help to return for the others. After seeing how she had performed, Mrs. Lowry said she and the two children would accompany her. They made their way through the jungle underbrush along the coast line of Sumatra, to Sunda Straits. There they bribed a native boatman to take them across the straits to Java.

Word of their arrival had somehow proceeded them, and they were captured by hostile natives. Knowing the Japs would pay a bounty for them dead or alive, the natives tied their hands behind their backs and started to execute them. They killed the two children first, and then turned to Margie. She showed no fear as a bolo knife severed her head almost clear of her body. As they turned to Mrs. Lowry, she broke and ran through their slashing knives, around the corner of a native hut and head-on into a waiting Jap patrol which saved her from certain death at the hands of the natives and brought her here for internment.

The morning after my conversation with Mrs. Lowry, we were kicked and aroused to our feet to begin our first day as an organized work party. Ten of us were lined up, counted, and lectured to in Japanese before we left the prison. They marched us out of the prison, and after winding down the crooked streets, we came to a large mansion-type home which the Japs had turned into their headquarters. Only high-ranking Japanese officers were housed here. A General Nickatoma was in charge. He was a short, stocky man with a large handlebar moustache and a very military bearing. His chest was covered with medals, including an American First World War citation.

He proceeded to lecture us in broken English, an indoctrination speech, mostly on the theory of Asia being for the Asiatics and if left to their own devices, they were

quite capable of handling the situation without the help
of Europe and America. He praised his own capabilities
to great heights and told us of the magnificent job he had
done here. To us, regular servicemen who knew the situation as it really was, his lecture was quite a farce. After he
finished, and amid bowing and scraping, they turned us
over to guards who put us to work moving supplies. We
had been detailed to carry large boxes of tea from a store-
house, down a steep outside stairs, to waiting trucks. The
boxes of tea were lightweight but big and bulky to handle.
In our working party was one very young boy. Talking to
him as we worked, we learned he was an Australian sail-
or by the name of Charlie Goodchap. He was eager to
talk about his adventures. He had started out at the age
of twelve as a cabin boy in the British and Australian Na-
vies, and had worked himself up to a torpedoman on the
light cruiser 'Perth,' which was sunk the same night our
ship went down. Goodchap had spent eighteen months
in action in the Mediterranean Sea with the number twelve
torpedo tube as a battle station. In all their actions, the
command "Cease Fire" had come before Goodchap had
a chance to fire his torpedo.

The night of their last battle, after abandon ship was
sounded, Goodchap was down in a lifeboat being held
alongside the sinking ship. In great Australian style he
yelled, "Hold it, you bloody bastards," climbed back aboard
the listing ship, jumped up on top of the torpedo tubes
and screamed, "Fire Twelve!" He fired his torpedo, and
then climbed back down into the lifeboat; he casually said,
"Well, what are you blokes waiting on?"

While he was telling this story, Goodchap was going
down the stairs a few steps in front of me, with a large box

of tea on his shoulder. With every step my toe came closer to his box of tea, and finally I could resist the urge no longer. Tapping the box with the tip of my toe, I sent it flying down the stairs. The four foot box of tea bounced and rolled down the steps, broke open, and hit a Jap guard, showering him with tea. Goodchap was trying to hold his balance on the steps and we were all having a good laugh. Of course, the Japs called Goodchap down, beat and slapped him around a little, but no one was seriously hurt in the fracas. Goodchap only laughed and took it all as a big joke. We realized how great he was, and good for our morale. We were all glad he was a member of our working party.

This first day, the Japs came out with large wooden buckets of steaming rice with a bucket of stewed fishheads as a side dish to feed us. Being as starved as we had been in prison on dirty rice balls, we thought we were being well-fed! The soup from the stewed fishheads at least had a taste and smelled good. While eating and talking, we decided that we were a lot better off than our shipmates back in the hell of their dank cells.

After a few more days of working and marching back and forth from the prison, we began to get sick and weak, and continually suffered from diarrhea. One morning, as our guards were walking us past the door of the Jap cook houses, someone suddenly grabbed hold of me and lifted me bodily through the door. I looked up and found myself in the grip of a large Jap. He looked like a monster - as big as any man I ever saw. He was at least six feet four inches tall, and weighed no less than three hundred pounds. He looked down at me and grinning, put me behind the door.

Upon reaching their destination, our guards discovered I was missing, and came back frantically screaming and searching for me. They came to the cook house door but after a lengthy discussion with my new captor, left and returned to work with only a nine man detail.

The big Jap cook came over, patted me on the head and smiled down at me. I didn't know what he wanted, but I began to realize that he was going to be friendly. Treating me as a guest of honor, he got a high-back chair for me to sit on. "You," he said, "Tocksong be oke," which I knew to the Japs meant very sick. He proceeded to tell me, in our crude way of conversing which included sign language, Japanese and a few words of English, that he had been watching me go to the toilet for two days and that he was going to cure my dysentery.

He handed me two large pills and a glass of water. Taking another look at this great hulk of Jap, I meekly took them. He stood over me, grinned, patted me on the head again, and set about to prepare a meal for me that I was to remember for a long time.

He went to a large upright refrigerator and took out what looked like the loin of a whole hog. Removing the tenderloin, he skillfully began to dice it into small cubes, placing them in a hot Ygon and frying them until they were a crisp golden brown. Being half-starved and always hungry, I found that the wonderful aroma from the cooking meat was almost more than I could endure.

Heaping it all in one large serving bowl and handing me a large spoon, he made motions for me to eat it. A more delectable dish I could never remember eating. I was so engrossed in eating, I didn't notice he was preparing another dish for me. Being so full I could hardly move, I was going to refuse the second dish, but I soon found out that he was insulted to think I wouldn't eat what he set before me. So, full or not, I proceeded to eat the second dish.

When I was through, we again began to converse in our haphazard way. Through what I managed to understand of our conversation and a few pictures he showed me, I found out he was a champion sumo wrestler in his home town. With a full stomach, I began to get drowsy, so smiling, he gave me three packages of cigarettes and a sack of fruit and took me out on the lawn to a shade tree. He told me to yasama (sleep).

When our guards saw me under this tree, a couple of them started toward us and I thought, "Well, this is it," but my new-found friend came to my rescue. He immediately began to bark orders at them and told them I was to do no more work that day, but just to sit under the tree and rest. Whether he had any authority or not, I didn't know, but they left me in peace.

Leaning against the tree half-asleep, I suddenly sensed something wrong. Looking up, I saw this immaculately dressed Jap officer standing over me. I got up and spoke to him, but he just looked at me with a blank stare. I decided to light a cigarette, so I offered him one, which in his understanding way, he refused. I didn't have a match, so I asked him for a light. He handed me a beautiful cigarette lighter and case that I immediately recognized as a Ronson, American made. Because of the poor fuel I guess, I couldn't get it in operation so I handed it back.

"These damn things are sure hard to keep in operation," he said. "Let's go inside and I'll get you some matches."

He turned and I followed. Upon arriving at the door we went down a long hall, through an archway, into the spacious living room of the former Dutch Adjutant, to a beautiful desk. Taking some matches from the desk, he lit my cigarette. As he did so I noticed he wore an American class ring on his finger. He saw me looking at it and he immediately turned it under.

I said, "You speak good American. Have you ever been to the States?"

He looked at me, starting jabbering in Japanese and quickly escorted me back outdoors. All the rest of the time I worked here, even while working for him, I never heard him speak another word of English.

It was while walking back to prison this particular night that I first saw Chee-Sigh, in all her shining glory. Blond shining curls, shining big blue eyes, and a radiant smile; even though she was only five years old. Riding by our Jap guards on bicycle, she seemed to express a courageous exuberance. I watched her very closely and saw that she had something she was trying to get to me. Circling down the street and back again, she defied the Jap guards, darted by me and slipped me three packs of cigarettes. She turned the corner, waved and disappeared.

Arriving back at prison we were greeted by a new Jap Sotjo (Sergeant) and also by our ship's doctor, Doctor Burroughs, better known to us as 'Butch.'

"Hi Dr. Burroughs, glad to see you out from behind bars. How'd you swing it?"

"I don't know; they said I was to be the prison doctor and take care of the sick and wounded. But I want you to know it's almost an impossibility because my hands are tied. I have nothing to work with."

"Don't worry, Doc, just remember your presence alone helps a lot of us."

"Well, I'm glad to hear that. You may help me with my first operation as soon as you eat your rice."

"Okay," I answered, "but who's sick?"

"Red Flowers. He has a bullet or piece of shrapnel in the back of his leg. I must try to get it out."

After an elaborate dinner consisting of one ball of gummy rice, I went over to see the "hospital" Dr. Burroughs had set up in a small cell. It consisted of a wooden table down the middle and one broken down chair which held his surgical instruments. A razor, a pair of pliers, and a few pieces of clean cloth he had scrounged someplace were all he had to work with.

"Well, you're just in time. Here they come with Red."

Looking back through the prison corridor, I saw two men approaching, supporting Red in between them, with an arm around each shoulder in the manner of football players helping an injured teammate off the field. It seemed that his one leg was useless. We helped him up on the table and laid him on his stomach. Doc had two of us on each side of him to help hold him if necessary. Then he proceeded to go to work on Red. The calf of his leg was badly swollen and inflamed. First he put a hand on each side and started to squeeze to remove some of the pus and corruption. The hole he got opened up in the calf was not big enough to allow the pliers to probe for the shrapnel, so he went to work with the straight razor. Finally he looked up smiling, with a small black object clasped in the pliers.

"Well, Red," he said, "if we got it all, and with the help of God, your leg will be o.k."

Red was carried back to his cell and the next patients were brought in; two men whose feet were nothing but solid blisters from running and walking on the hot blacktop roads before they were captured. They could not walk or even stand on their feet. We placed them on the table and Doc went to work with the razor. He cut and peeled the bottom layers of hide from their feet to relieve the pus and pressure. When he finished their feet looked like bloody pulp, but they both said they felt better.

Feeling a little green around the gills, I returned to my cell and sacked out for the night. The next thing I knew I was being kicked to my feet to go to work although it was before daylight. Our guards put us in two ranks of five and marched us back to the Jap headquarters. We arrived early and had to wait under a tree until time to go to work. While we were waiting, a scrawny, sickly-looking Jap with buck teeth came up to me, took me by the hand, and led me behind a small garage-like building. He motioned for me to sit down on a small stack of straw in the sunshine. Reaching in his pocket, he took out a drinking glass and handed it to me. From his other pocket he took out three duck eggs and broke them into the glass. Taking the glass and spoon, he proceeded to beat the eggs until they were a frothing mass. Handing the glass back to me, he motioned for me to drink it, but I refused. He jumped up, let out a squeak, jerked out his bayonet, and rapped me across the shoulder. I immediately changed my mind; I held my breath and gulped down the stinking mess.

About this time our regular guards began yelling for us to fall in, and told us we were going someplace else to work. We marched back by the prison into a residential district, to a house surrounded by barbed wire. It was our job to clear it of all furnishings and get it ready for its new occupants. Just as we had finished, Jap trucks pulled up, loaded with the women and children from our prison. After about forty days in their cells, they were a disheveled lot.

Their guards herded them inside the barbed wire enclosure and proceeded to tell them this was their new home and also that they were free to come and go as they pleased, that the fence was only for their protection. God knows they needed it; for the ones with no money with which to buy food were told they might live with a Jap officer to earn their keep. Their immediate reactions were of almost complete hysteria and resentfulness. But I later heard that those who refused or who were rejected by the Jap officers were turned over to the Imperial Army as prostitutes.

As they marched us back to prison in a round-about way to display us to the natives more or less, we crossed a small bridge with a stream of water beneath. Through sign language to the Jap in charge, I got permission for us to take a bath in the stream. Even though it was filthy with debris, my body seemed to crave the soaking I gave it in this stream. I sure felt refreshed. But hungry! God, won't they ever give us anything decent to eat?

Arriving back at prison we were met by the Jap Sergeant in charge who was all smiles. I casually remarked,

"Look at that bastard, grinning like a possum eating shit. He probably just got permission to kill us."

Instead, he told us through an interpreter that when the sun came up tomorrow morning, we would be transferred to a Prison of War camp at Batavia, Java. There we would receive good food and clothing and have spacious living quarters.

"Well," I remarked, "nothing can be worse than this, so let's go get a good night's rest and be prepared for what may come tomorrow."

That night I prayed and thanked God for our unfortunate friends who would get out of their crowded cells for the first time since the doors had been locked forty-seven days ago.

6

New Surroundings

Tired as we were, no one got any sleep that night because our anxiety had risen so high with the expectation of moving. Bright and early the next morning we heard the welcome roar of trucks outside the prison wall. All night long we had been wondering how long a walk it might be to Batavia.

They made us squat down in the truck beds so crowded together we could barely move. In each corner was a guard with a rifle and bayonet and on each cab was mounted a machine gun. Soon we were all loaded and on our way. Such a wild ride we never had! We arrived at our destination before sundown, hot, dusty, and thirsty. As we climbed out of the trucks, we found we could hardly stand up, let alone walk.

Upon marching into the camp, the first thing we saw was a sign that said, "Bicycle Camp Batavia," on the Guardhouse. A wide street ran down the middle of the camp with barracks off to each side. Each barracks was surrounded with barb-wire, to form a compound for each group.

They divided us into groups according to nationalities and marched us to our new quarters. In the barracks next to us we soon found there were more Americans. They were from the 131st Field Artillery, Texas National Guard. Immediately we milled together and started talking over our experiences together. These soldiers had all their equipment and clothing which they readily shared with us. We were so happy to have something decent to wear we almost cried. Their generosity led them to share everything they had with us. It seemed almost unbelievable.

We immediately set about to prepare our living quarters as best we could. The barracks were divided into cubicles. There were four of us in my cubicle: "Bull" Barbetti, "Doc" Willis, "Whitney" Axelson and myself.

We didn't have time to get settled before the welcome shout: "Chow down!" As we made our way to the far corner of the camp for our food, greetings were so numerous and such a mixture of nationalities represented that it seemed like the League of Nations. The smell from the kitchen made my nostrils twitch with anticipation. When I reached the head of the line to receive my rice, the Australian cook serving the food exclaimed:

"Blimey! Look at the blooming billy this bloody Yank has."

I realized he was talking about my mess kit, which was a large hubcap I had gotten from a car at a Jap motor pool in Serang.

"O.K., Snowy," he said. "Hold her over the barrel and

we'll fill 'er up."

By the time I walked away from there he must have had a gallon of rice stacked on my plate, topped with a dipper of fish and seaweed stew.

"Snowy," he said, "if that ain't enough, you come back for seconds, and I'll give you more. Don't you worry, son, we'll fatten you up."

By the time I'd finished my meal I was really full. My stomach felt as if it was bloated. I just seemed dazed and doped as I waddled back to my quarters. As I neared the main thoroughfare in camp, I was approached by a small "Aussie."

"Hey, Cobber," he said. "Are you sure you can make it?"

"Yeah, I reckon," I said.

He introduced himself to me as Tom George, age fifty-five, of the Royal Australian Army. Then he wanted to know all about me. As best I could, I proceeded to tell him the events of my past up to now.

When we arrived at our barracks I began to feel a little better so we sat down on the veranda steps to shoot the breeze.

"Snowy," he says, "I don't want you to take this wrong, but I want to give you a little fatherly advice. She's going to be a long hard pull, son, before they get us out of this mess. It will be a dog eat dog, and survival of the fittest. So just remember, son, don't worry about no bloody bastard but yourself. Ask no quarter and give none. As far as these little yellow slant-eyed bastards are concerned, don't do nothing for them unless they got a bayonet in your back, because they'll let you work yourself to death. I know you believe in God, but just remember you'll have to lie, cheat, steal, and maybe even kill to get out of here. Don't you worry though, the good Lord will forgive you. Well, I must be going Snowy, the yellow bastards will be around to count us in a little while. Come over to my place when you get a chance, and meet my cobber. His name's Mick Conry. Just come in the barracks and ask, everybody knows me and Mick. So long, Snowy," he waved as he turned the corner leaving our compound.

I was amazed at the calm way he accepted being a prisoner, and decided then and there if I expected to survive I'd have to be the same way.

7

Making a Buck

"Fall in!" I heard someone shout, and looked to see Lt. Hamlin standing in the middle of the compound. We started struggling to our feet and congregating in front of the barracks. Boy, what a disheveled mess we were! In all there were about three hundred and sixty survivors from our ship. All shapes and sizes, ages and forms. We could not recognize many of our close friends because of their horrible condition, and what they had been through. After the Japs counted us and dismissed us, we shot the breeze awhile and then sacked out.

The next morning the Japs told us we'd get a day or two of rest before we would have to go to work. My cellmates and I immediately took a tour of the camp to see what we could gather up to make us some bunks. We managed to get a few pieces of wood, some rice sacks, bamboo poles, and carried them back to our cells. I borrowed some wire cutters from a soldier and cut some strands from the fence with which to wire our bunks together. While doing so, I unconsciously picked up a small piece of barbed wire and started clipping it with the cutters. As I gazed at the pieces, an idea suddenly struck. I heard the Englishmen over in their barracks saying they had cigarettes, lighters, and petrol for them, but no flints. These cuttings looked like flints. Just maybe they would be sucker enough to buy some! Better yet, I could cut some to uniform size. This I very patiently did, until I had three hundred pieces cut. I managed to get hold of some white tissue paper and wrapped them three pieces to the package.

I borrowed a lighter from a soldier, tested it to see that it would light, stuffed the small packages in my pocket, and casually ambled over to the English compound. I went to the very back of their barracks to start my sales, planning to work my way back to the entrance before they discovered the flints would not spark. The sales were great, but I knew I couldn't waste time getting out of here. I sold my packages at first for fifty cents or the equivalent in any kind of currency they happened to have. As soon as I saw they didn't complain, I raised the price to one Dutch Guilder. I was just about through the barracks when I heard my first complaint from the rear. I politely excused myself and told them I would return soon. I was only a few yards away when it sounded like their roof was coming off. I ran back to my own compound and got lost in the crowd which had gathered to see what was the matter. Not only was I fifty or sixty dollars richer, but I had also had a good laugh, which is invaluable when you're confined.

No one has to tell you when you have done wrong, because deep in your heart you know you have. Praying to God that night, I asked His forgiveness, but all the time in the back of my mind, I could hear old Tom George's words, "You're gonna have to lie, steal and cheat, maybe even kill, to get out of here."

The next morning they had us fall out to go to work. As we got to the Guardhouse, they cut off about fifteen of us, and one officer, a no good son-of-a-bitch by the name of John Bell. We climbed aboard a truck and they took us to a motor pool they had set up on a golf course. All morning long we pushed and shoved cars and trucks around, and rolled fifty gallon gasoline drums. At noon our guards marched us over to their quarters to feed us. They let us sit in the shade across a driveway by a tree-row. They fed us some watery fish stew with our rice. We were a little strange to the Japs yet, so they'd still gather around us and chatter like monkeys in a zoo. While we were still relaxing after eating, John Bell, being the no-good bastard he was, began to carry on a conversation with a Jap Sergeant. At the end of the talk I heard John Bell saying, "Yeah, in fact, I know I could whip any six Japs your size."

The Jap didn't say anything. He just grinned, turned, and left. Of course, John Bell crowed like a rooster, but his glory was short-lived. The doors of a one-car garage suddenly burst open and out came the Jap wearing only a G-string. Behind him stood five well-built little Japs, also grinning. He invited John Bell into the garage very politely. When he refused, the guards made him go. They closed the door so we couldn't see in, and then proceeded to work John over. He didn't last very long. A few minutes later, when they opened the door and threw him out, we thought he was dead. He was just a bloody pulp all over.

We carried him back to camp that night, but we didn't think he'd live long. But, after a few weeks he was up and about again.

After John Bell's foolish beating they changed our work details, and I was assigned with four others on what we called the "gas robbers crew." A Jap Sergeant, a guard, and a truck driver would drive us around the city until we spotted a gasoline station. Then we'd pump out the gasoline into barrels on the back of the truck, and haul it back to the Jap fuel depot.

During my second day on this detail, I again saw Chee-Sigh riding her bike as before. Across the street though, was this white lady immaculately dressed in a white tropical suit. She seemed to be with Chee-Sigh; I saw her talking to the little girl so I thought to myself it was probably her mother. Chee-Sigh came across the street and asked the Jap guard if she might give me some cigarettes and fruit she had in the basket on the front of her bike. He said, "O.K.", so she came over to me and told me in broken English that the lady across the street would like to talk to me. I asked the guard if it would be alright. At first he stubbornly refused, but after I slipped him a couple of bills he said, "O.K."

I went around behind the station and met a young lady.

"Hi," she said. "Are you an American?"

"Yes, but you don't have to tell me you are; you're from Brooklyn. What in the name of God are you doing here? Especially dressed like this?"

"Well, I was a newspaper correspondent for a New York paper, and got trapped out here, so there was nothing I could do but pose as being Dutch. When they released the Dutch women they released me also. I have money and hope to make contact with someone to get me out of here."

"I guess you know what happens to these white women when they run out of money, so if you're not careful they'll have you working as a prostitute or living with a Jap officer to earn your keep."

"Not me, before I'd go to bed with one of those yellow dogs, I'd kill myself." She replied with such vehemence that I was afraid the guard would hear her.

"Here comes the guard, you better take off," I warned.

"O.K., but don't worry. I'll see you again. Take this money, it may help you. Don't say no, because there's more where it came from." Handing me two twenty dollar bills folded together, she disappeared around the corner.

"Thanks," I gulped.

When I got back to work the rumors were flying hot and fast as to who my new found friend was, where she came from and what she was doing here. For the next three days, I watched for her, but I never saw her again.

8

The Whiskey Racket

The following Monday I was assigned to a new working party and sent to the docks to load ships with supplies and loot to be sent to Japan. We were out on a long pier with warehouses down the middle. Our guards were stationed at the pier gates, so their surveillance of us was not too close. In all there were about 125 in our working party - Dutch, English, Australian and American. Getting permission to go to the toilet, I started down the opposite side of the dock. As I approached a Jap merchant ship, I saw a little Jap in a sailor hat, stooping down on the edge of the pier and fishing for something.

My curiosity got the better of me, so I went over and stooped down alongside of him. He looked over and grinned and pointed down below. On the bottom were numerous bottles which the tide had carried in from all the sunken ships in the harbor. They contained Johnny Walker whiskey and Gordon's Dry Gin. He had been fishing them out with a wire and selling them to the Jap sailors and soldiers on the ships above us.

I immediately made motions to him that I'd dive in and get more for him. It seemed to be agreeable to him, so in I went. When I came up, I had a whole case of whiskey still in its wooden crate. He helped me get it up on the dock, and we set up shop. He had been charging the Japs fifty cents a bottle. I immediately raised the price to one dollar. They didn't complain so I raised it to five dollars a bottle, then ten. Before we finished we were charging them twenty-five dollars a bottle. I also borrowed two large English packs and filled them as full of bottles as I could. In the two, I got forty-eight bottles of whiskey and four quarts of Gordon's Dry Gin. These I hid in the warehouse. By this time I was tired of diving, so we closed shop. I took my new-found friend into the warehouse and we divided the money. I put all the small bills in his stack and all the big bills in mine, and he seemed perfectly happy. I guess neither of us had ever had so much money before. I hid mine in my pants and milled back into the working party.

Before we left camp that morning, they had given us twenty dollars apiece in Jap script money. If we possibly could, we were to buy anything from the natives which might be useful in our camp kitchen. Knowing that our guards probably wouldn't search us when we got back to camp, I offered an Australian a bottle of whiskey to carry a pack into camp for me. He readily agreed. I had a few anxious moments when we were counted in by the guardhouse, but we made it without a hitch. After we were safely in my cubicle, I paid the Aussie his bottle, thanked him, and unloaded the rest into my bunk. I had gambled and it had paid off.

As soon as the rest of the working party came in, I got Bull to guard my loot, went to the Australian barracks, and invited Tom and Mick over for a party. We drank very little because we knew we couldn't afford to get caught. In the next couple of hours I had unlimited offers from people wanting to buy a bottle. I had plenty of money now, so I decided to hold out for a while.

The next day I bought my way onto an inside work detail, the street sweepers gang. The only work we did was sweep down the main street for about two blocks each morning. The rest of the day I'd just roam around the camp buying or selling all kinds of loot. I'd already decided if anyone was going to prosper from this racketeering, it was going to be me. This was a heck of a lot better than sweating my can outside for the damned Japs.

Hearing a commotion outside, I went out to see what was going on. A Jap was nailing a large order on the side of the building. It stated that we were going to be questioned very soon, and that we must tell the truth, that if we didn't, we would be very severely punished. He had hardly finished before they called us out to be questioned. My name was close to the top of the list, and therefore I was close to the front of the line for questioning. As I stood between the guards, I wondered what information I could ever give them that would be of any use to their war effort. The next thing I knew, I received a rap from the guard beside me as he said "Oosh" move on. I was taken inside the office and sat at a table across from the two high-ranking Jap officers I had never seen before, and their interpreter.

He looked at me and said, "Namo Condy."

I replied, "Yes."

"Where you from?"

I said, "Chicago," knowing they thought everyone from there was a gangster. Sometimes it was enough to make them let you alone.

"Now you must tell the truth, understand?"

I nodded the affirmative, and he began again.

"We want to know, if Nippon lands in Chicago, will the roads there be strong, to hold up our tanks."

Holding up four fingers on each hand and making a traveling motion I said, "Oh yes, we got roads this wide." Then, indicating the height of the table, I added, "Concrete that thick."

"Oh! Osoaka, you go now." I guess I told them what they wanted to hear, so I was allowed to return to my barracks.

When I returned, I decided to take a bath, so I went out to the bath tongs, which was only a square cement tank with an apron around it to stand on and wash. I was near the back fence where they had some high ranking Dutch officers locked up. I had just finished washing when I heard someone call, "Hey Yank!"

I looked up and saw this tall dignified looking guy on the other side, so I walked over to the fence to talk to him.

"Are you the boy who got all the whiskey into camp the other day?"

"I might be. Why?"

"Well you know I'm Dutch and I've always been a heavy drinker. I'd like to buy some from you."

"Save your money, mister, I don't need it. Maybe later."

"Oh, you don't understand. Money is no object, I have a whole bag full, I'll pay you anything you want."

"Sorry, I'm not interested." I turned and walked back toward my quarters.

Someone walked up alongside me and said, "Do you know who that was?"

"No, who?"

"Hell, he's the Dutch Air Marshal General."

"So what? I'm Nick Day."

"Yeah, but they say they are going to execute that poor bastard. They've already been torturing him."

"Well, that being the case, I'll just give him some whiskey."

Going back to my bunk I got two bottles, wrapped them in a shirt, returned to the fence and called for the General. He came out and I said, "Hey, here's a present for you." He looked as though he was going to cry with joy. He thanked me no less than a dozen times.

By this time in the evening, it was time for "tinko" or muster, so we lounged around the compound waiting for the Japs to come and count us. With them this particular evening they had a new officer, who they told us was going to take charge of our camp. He made it understood to Lt. Hamlin that we must wear our hair just like his. Removing his hat he showed us his head was shaved. He also said he'd give us barber scissors and razors with which to do the job, and that we must have it done before "tinko" tomorrow.

Of course all of us being typical Americans, we went to the extreme, shaved eyebrows and all. The white heads against our tanned skins looked like a snowball on a coalpile. The next evening while waiting on the Japs for "tinko", we discussed all the oddball shapes of the skulls and were having quite a time when the Japs got there for the count. Lt. Hamlin stood in front in his most military manner, saluted the Japs, did an about face to us and barked, "Rackem-up!" Of course we all laughed, but the Japs couldn't understand what was funny. It seemed the more Lt. Hamlin tried to explain, the less they understood. They kept us standing there at attention for about four hours until we finally quieted down. They left the compound shaking their heads in disgust and jabbering to themselves, still not knowing what was funny.

While I was in this camp, I managed to scrounge forty or fifty feet of electric wire and an old socket with no switch. By snitching a bulb from one of the fixtures at the top of the barracks, I rigged a light in my cubicle. By shielding the fixture with a shirt, we could play cards after lights out.

Everything went well for about a week. Then, early one morning, as I was scrubbing the floor, "The Basher" entered. (Our nicknames for the guards were carefully chosen and served as a code to warn fellow prisoners of sadistic tendencies, or other quirks.) The shirt we had been using to shield the light had somehow gotten misplaced. I must have glanced up at the fixture with a nervous, guilty look because "The Basher" also looked up and immediately saw my makeshift wiring job.

"Joe-toe," he said, which meant "good." Then he reached up and took hold of the socket. You could almost see his ears light up. The floor was wet from my scrubbing, and the current knocked him all the way across the cubicle.

He got up and called in two more guards from the outside. Then he made me understand that I was to take down the fixture, right now. I climbed up in the rafters and jerked the wire loose from the hot line outside. As I continued to tear it down, he proceeded to coil it around his forearm from the elbow to palm. He left enough loose end to whip a handle around the coil. When he's finished this, I thought he was through with me, but it was only the beginning.

He made me take off my clothes and stand at attention. Then he started beating me with the wire. After the first few lashes, I seemed numb to my toes. Then I saw a blinding flash, and that was all.

I came to that afternoon, a mass of welts and razor-like cuts all down my body. Behind my right ear was a large knot. The socket had hit me there, knocking me out. No one showed me any sympathy. When we first became prisoners, we would raise hell because the Japs beat someone; but as time wore on, we would just give them a passing glance and say:

"Wonder what that stupid jerk did to get the Nips on his back." As long as you didn't get caught breaking the rules, you were O.K., but you never seemed to know what their rules were. They seemed to change with every change of the guard. The smart thing to do was learn the whims of each guard, then judge yourself accordingly. We had each nicknamed to sound warning to others like, "Basher," "Monk," "Donald Duck," "Sweet Pea," and many others.

It was always amazing to me how well the names fit the personalities.

Recuperation from my beating was a slow and agonizing process. Of course, the Japs didn't let us miss any work if we were able to be on our feet at all. Maybe it was better this way, because you couldn't just lie around and feel sorry for yourself.

"I wonder where they are taking us today. They surely can't have much work for us to do, there's only ten of us in this truck." Arriving at a Jap motor pool we were taken to a large shed alongside a Jap parade ground and drill field. In the shed were piles of American-made truck parts. We were to sort them into crates and prepare them for shipment to Japan. We were sitting in a circle sorting the parts when the Japs on the drill field were dismissed. They all congregated around us in a huge mob, peering at us and jabbering in excitement. I guess we were the first American prisoners they had seen, so we were really the center of attraction.

About this time the Jap in charge of us burst in, screaming at us in Japanese. We just looked at him. Then someone said, "I wonder what that stupid bastard wants."

A little Jap standing behind me spoke in perfect English and said, "A truck is stalled out there, and he wants you to come and push it. Go ahead, and when you get back, I'd like to talk to you."

When we had pushed the truck out of the way and returned to our sorting, he chased the other Japs away and squatted down alongside me to talk. He removed his hat revealing long hair. I thought this very odd, so I asked him about it.

"Oh," he said, "I'm not in the army. I'm a civilian interpreter attached to General Nicotoma's staff." He added, "Say, is there anything I can do for you guys?"

"Anything!" I said, "Buddy, you can do everything. We haven't had a decent meal for weeks. Maybe you can rustle us up something decent to eat."

"I'll see what I can do."

At noon he returned with two little Japs each carrying two large wooden buckets. Two were full of rice, the other two contained a real good fish stew. We ate until we were full, then lay down in the shade. Sitting down alongside me, the interpreter handed me three packs of cigarettes.

"Is there anything else you really need?"

"Oh yes," I said, "I could sure use a toothbrush and some tooth powder; maybe even a little sugar to go on that lousy rice in camp." He didn't say anything, just got up and left.

That afternoon as we were preparing to go back to camp, he returned, handing me a rice sack about one-third full of stuff.

"This is real nice of you, but I can't get it by the guard-house at camp."

"Here, take this note and when you get there, show it to the guard in charge."

I had no trouble getting into camp, and was met by my buddy Tony.

"In case you ain't heard," he said, "we are going to

move. You had better get rid of the rest of that whiskey."

"When we leaving, where we going?"

"We're leaving tomorrow morning but we don't know for sure where we're going, maybe Japan."

"Well, there's just one thing to do. I'll try to dump the rest of that whiskey on those Dutch officers."

"Save some for us. We'll have a little party tonight."

I took two bottles apiece down to Dr. Burroughs and Dr. Epstein at the camp hospital. "Here," I said with a wink," This is for medicinal purposes only."

Returning to my quarters, I put all but three bottles in a bag and headed for the Dutch officers' camp. When I called for the old Dutch Air Marshal General, he was very happy to see me and acted as though he was waiting for me. He handed me a package of money and I could tell right away it was quite a sizable sum; about twenty-five hundred dollars in their money. That night we had a little farewell get-together with the friends we had made in this camp, because we didn't know whether or not we would ever see them again.

9

Surgery in Singapore

Bright and early the next morning, we were on our way
to the docks to be loaded aboard ship. As we marched up
to this old tramp steamer the Japs were using to transport
us, I noticed the name on her stern. MOGI MARU. They
loaded us into the forward hold like cattle. They had installed tiers of wooden planking from the overhead to the
deck like shelves in a dark fruit cellar. We were made to
lay back on the shelves with our heads to the middle. It
was so crowded you couldn't move or turn over. The stench
was horrible; we had no toilet facilities other than half of a
wooden barrel sitting out in the middle. Of course, we had
many ill among us with dysentery and other tropical diseases,
not to mention the sea sickness.

Immediately we started to talk to the guards to try to
bribe our way topside to get a little fresh air. At least if we
could get our sick up there we could have a little more
room, and also somewhat more sanitary conditions below.

Our second day aboard they finally decided to feed us and let us come up for air. As I climbed up the wooden ladder to the main deck, the tropic sun seemed to blind me, but after the stifling hold, even the hot, humid tropic air seemed cooling and refreshing. They lined us up around the deck to feed us, and brought out huge wooden tubs of steaming rice, green in color. They gave us all the curried rice we wanted, but our only other food was one piece of slimy cooked seaweed that had a fish flavor.

They let us stay on deck until almost dark, but they kept guards stationed all around us with rifles and machine guns; days and nights were endless on this trip. At least no one died on the way, which was very unusual as we were to find out.

Speculation ran high as to where we were going. While we were sitting topside I said to Lt. Hamlin, "Boy, this ole tub sure is a bucket of bolts."

"That's not all either, son," he replied. "Take a look around you. Do you notice there are no brass fittings of any kind on this ship? She's got quite a history, though. She's one of the ships we captured from the Germans during World War I. Later she was sold to Japan for scrap iron, and now here she is being used as a troop ship by Japan."

"Well, I guess that's better than making bombs out of her."

"Maybe she will stay afloat until we reach our destination. The scuttlebutt is that we're going to Singapore, there is supposedly a large camp there. We've been making about four knots. We'll probably get there sometime tonight or early tomorrow morning."

"That being the case, I'm going below and sack out. We'll probably have a long walk when we get there."

The anticipation of arriving in Singapore made all efforts to sleep practically nil, so as the sun came up, I gathered together my meager personal belongings and climbed top-side to wait. The water had a mirror-like calmness about it this morning, and a few miles distant off our port bow, were some beautiful green colored tropical islands.

We made port before noon and tied up at the docks in Singapore. The docks themselves were not too war-worn; but in the distance I could see that the causeway had quite a gap in it. As we fell in on the docks, I noticed a lot of other prisoners working nearby. The usual vulgar salutations were exchanged and we started our march. Ordinarily when the Japs marched us we would walk or run fifty minutes and rest ten; but today our guards seemed to be in a hurry to get rid of us, so it was non-stop for about three or four hours. The going got rougher as we progressed, because the roads got very hilly and mountainous. Coming up a long steep hill, off to the right in the distance, I saw the prison.

"Oh no!" I said to no one in particular, "Not another one of those filthy holes. We'll be dying off like flies." Thank God my fears were shortlived. We marched by the gates of the prison to a barracade in the road, and a Jap guardhouse. Stretching as far as I could see in each direction were double fence rows of coiled barbed wire.

We thought we had reached our destination, but found out we had about five more miles to go. The Japs had taken the south end of the island and just cut it off as a prison camp. Part of it had been an English Army camp, and we found this was where we were to live. All told, the Japs had about sixty-five thousand prisoners of all nationalities here.

Our quarters were on the extreme southern tip of the island, up on the top of a high hill. The building was three stories high, made of concrete with red tile roofing. We had a toilet with running water on each floor, verandas all around, and a cookhouse outside.

After talking the situation over, Bull Barbetti, Whitey Axelson and I decided we'd stay outside on the veranda. It would be cooler than living inside.

"Well, there's one thing about it, we sure have a beautiful view from here, and that breeze from off the Bay feels good."

We were no more than settled when the compound, "Fall-in" was given. Colonel Thorpe, our senior officer, gave us the rules of the camp.

"First of all men, gather around in a circle here, so you can all hear. Now I want you to know the English are in charge of the camps, so any rations we receive must come through them. I asked about our Red Cross supplies, and they told me they had been shipped onto Burma, our next port of call. Plenty for them, but none for us; but remember, we are all in this together, and I don't want you to go off half-cocked and get yourselves in trouble. You are Americans, and I expect you to act as such. As long as you do what's right and conduct yourselves in a gentlemanly way, I'll back you up one hundred per cent. Good luck and fall out!"

"Hey Whitey, how about those Limey bastards keeping all them American Red Cross supplies and us with nothing to eat but this damned ole dirty rice."

"Don't worry, if they got it, we'll get it, by hook or crook. They'll get up mighty damn early in the morning to out-smart us."

The rest of the day we spent just wandering about the camp, more or less casing the place. That night a few of us were holding a little conference around my bunk, when up strolls Dempsey Key.

"Man," he said, "I can taste that good ole southern fried chicken. I was just up there by that English General's head-quarters, and he has a chicken coop alongside with about twenty chickens just right for frying. I need one volunteer to hold the sack. I'll get the chickens."

"Dempsey," I said, "do you think we could get away with it?"

"Man! Don't you all know I was the best chicken thief in Texas before the war? When ah steals a chicken, you can't even hear a feather rustle."

We crept quietly up the hill to the back of General Black-borne's quarters, and Dempsey went to work like an old hand. First he took a pair of wire cutters and cut the wire on the back side of the pen.

"That's my escape hole in case I get caught inside the pen. You all hold the sack just inside the hole."

On the way back home I said, "Dempsey, I never thought it possible for anyone to steal that many chickens without even a squawk."

"Ah, it's nothing. I just tuck their heads under their wings, turn them upside down and put them in the sack."

Our cooks had everything in order for our midnight chicken fry. After the cleaning and dressing of nineteen chickens, we had quite a large pile of feathers and scraps. Everyone was jubilantly rejoicing over Dempsey's success on the chicken raid when up walked Colonel Thorpe and two or more of our officers.

"Hmmm," he said, "what goes on here? It sure smells good."

"Will you do us the honor, Colonel? And try the first piece?"

"Fine," he said, "fine."

"Colonel," Dempsey said, "please don't blame Nick and me. We was just walkin' up dis here road and dem birds jumped right in our sack."

We finished our party and buried all the bones, feathers, and evidence from our party and hid the sacks. I felt I could sleep forever on my full stomach. It seemed I had just gone to sleep when I heard someone yelling.

"All right, you guys, hit the deck!"

Rousing up from our slumber to fall in, the first thing I saw was General Blackborne and his staff. You could tell just from his looks that he was fuming mad.

All the innocents who had nothing to do with the chickens wondered what all the fuss was about, but to some of us, there was no doubt about what was going on.

"Well," said Colonel Thorpe as he saluted the General, "To what do we owe the unexpected pleasure of this visit so early in the morning?"

"Last evening someone stole away with my chickens, and I'm making a tour of the camp to try to find evidence of the culprits."

"Well, you're certainly welcome to search our compound if you like. I'd be very glad to accompany you."

The General started his tour and Colonel Thorpe casually fell in alongside him. I couldn't hear their conversation as they walked into our cookhouse, but as they came out Colonel Thorpe took out his handkerchief and wiped his mouth, looked at us, winked, grinned, walked to the gate of the compound, and saluted the General as he left. We knew the General must have known by the uproar of laughter and the typical military remarks that we had stolen his chickens, but he couldn't find the evidence. We were all proud of Colonel Thorpe for his diplomatic way of handling the General. The more we talked, the more our egos were inflated to think we had outsmarted him.

Someone casually remarked, "Well, maybe that will teach the Limey bastard a lesson that he ain't going to screw us out of our chow and get away with it." But the matter was not allowed to rest. Tension was still mounting, and it looked as though all hell was going to break loose.

Whitey walked up and said, "Hey Nick, let's take a stroll down through the camp and see how we can make out." Following a blacktop road down through the camp, we came upon a working party of Australians moving some

English officers from one building to another about four blocks away.

When we found out what they were doing, Whitey said, "Come on, Nick." We barged into an English Major's quarters and I said, "O.K., does all this junk go? If so, get out of our way so we can get it moved and over with.". Dis-assembling the bed, we took it out into the street and put it together again.

The bed had rollers, so Whitey said, "Climb aboard, Mate, I'll give you a ride." He pushed me to the bottom of the hill that led to our barracks, then I got off to help push. When we arrived at our bunksite, we had a crowd gathered around talking about our bed and testing the mattress.

As I lay down on the bed that night I said, "Whitey, do you think that Limey officer will come after his bed?"

"No, I don't think he'd have guts enough to. Besides this stuff no longer belongs to them. It belongs to the Japs." I sure must have slept soundly that night, because when I awoke the next morning, beds had sprung up like mushrooms all through our building.

Three or four days later, I woke one morning violently ill with severe pains in my stomach. Whitey and Bull helped me down to Dr. Lumpkin's quarters, and he told me the sad news.

"Nick son, I'm afraid you have acute appendicitis. I'll send you to the camp hospital and see what they say."

They got me to the hospital a couple of hours later, and a puny-looking English captain came in and examined me. He told me I'd have to have an operation immediately because if it ruptured before they got it out, I'd surely die.

That afternoon they took me down to the operating room, and I got my first glimpse of the surgeon who was going to operate on me. He was a Russian by the name of Desavonoff. He looked more like a tackle for the Chicago Bears than a surgeon. He spoke no English, so all conversation with him was nil.

The room was filthy by any standards, and it didn't look like they had much equipment.

"What kind of anesthetic you going to use?" I said.

An Australian standing alongside the wall said, "Don't worry, mate, we'll take care of you. We're your anesthetic."

I got the weak trembles when I realized they were going to operate on me without any anesthetic. The Australian said, "It's alright, Cobber, we'll take care of you; it will all be over in a few minutes."

I climbed on the table and stretched out, and they all gathered around to hold me. I opened my mouth to say something, but words wouldn't come out. They jammed a towel or something into my mouth, and said, "Bite this."

Dr. Desavonoff laid a heavy hand on my stomach, and it felt like it covered my whole abdomen. He started out with swift, sure strokes of the razor. I prayed to God, "Please, just let me pass out," but I couldn't. I saw stars, flashes of lightning, and perspired profusely.

"Thank God he's sewing me up," I thought. "I hope it won't take long. That's funny, my stomach doesn't hurt anymore. Who is that wiping the sweat off my face?"

They pried my jaws open and removed the towel. It made my mouth feel big and my head hollow. Dr. Desavonoff slapped me on the belly, looked down at me, and grinned.

"O.K.," he said. I guess that was a signal for them to take me out, because they loaded me on a stretcher and started up some steps with me.

The last thing I remember thinking was, "My God, am I dying, going to sleep, or passing out?"

I came to in complete darkness and heard someone say, "Are you awake, Snowy?"

I answered, "Yes, where am I?"

"On the third floor of the hospital barracks. We're glad to see you come around O.K."

I felt something crawling on my legs and ran my hand down to see what it was. When I brought my hand back up, I had a handful of bed bugs. I yelled and raised Cain until a Limey orderly appeared at the foot of my bed. "Get me out of these damn bed bugs," I said. "They're eating me alive. I got whelps all over me."

"Oh, but we can't do that. You see we're not allowed to move you without the doctor's permission."

"Get out of here then, you Limey bastard, I'll get away from them myself." He left with the light, and the bugs started crawling again. I rolled to the side of the bed and got my feet on the floor, my hands on the floor, and my butt on the bed. I was so weak I could neither get down nor up.

"Hey, Aussie, give me a hand will you?" I yelled.

"What's the matter Yank?", he said, lifting me in his

arms. "Where you want to go!"

"Anyplace," I said, "just get me away from these filthy bed bugs."

"All these beds are loaded with them, Snowy."

The hell with the beds, just put me out there on the veranda on the floor." He laid me down on the hard concrete, and sat down alongside.

"I'll kill the Limey so-and-so who tries to put me back in one of those bug-infested beds."

I laid around on the floor for three or four days, just shooting the bull and playing cards. During the morning rounds one morning, Dr. Desavanoff stopped to have a look at me. He removed the wrapping they had around me and looked at my side, and motioned for me to get up and walk. I wasn't too steady, but I could at least navigate. He grinned at me and said something to the interpreter in Russian. He in turn said to me, "The doctor says you'll be o.k. now, you can return to your own quarters."

"Tell him I said thanks a million. I hope someday I can do something for him."

I left the hospital right after our noon day rice and started the long slow walk back to the American compound, when I heard someone call, "Hey, Nick, wait up!"

I looked up and here came "Pappy Star" around the side of a hill. Pappy had been in the Navy about twelve years and was still a seaman first class. He had lost his false teeth when the ship went down, so he wasn't too much on looks at present.

"Come and see what I found," he said. "How do you

feel? I hope you're able to climb. Look." He was pointing down the side of the hill to a grove of coconut trees. Arriving at the trees, we soon discovered they were forty or fifty feet high and loaded with coconuts.

"Pappy," I said, "we'll never be able to climb them; you're too old and I'm too weak. What we need is a saw."

"You're right," he said. "Wait here; I'll be back in a little while with a saw." I leaned back against the tree and waited. About thirty minutes later I saw Pappy coming with something on his shoulder. When he arrived, he had a crosscut saw and an ax. He had taken them from an English woodshed.

We only had to cut down a few trees to get more coconuts than we would carry. To make a quick get-away, we tied them all together to be dragged. When we arrived at our barracks, we were greeted by a mob of other Americans wanting to know how we got the nuts. When we told them our story and where we hid the saw and the ax, they all took off to the trees. For hours we could hear the cry of "TIMBER!" and the crash of trees falling. Of course, we were dressed down by the English for destroying the King's property; they just couldn't concede the fact that it no longer belonged to him, but to the Japs. They again increased their military police force inside the camp to protect their trees. We only laughed and said,

"How dumb can the Strategic Retreat Artists get? All they'd have to do to get along with us is share the American Red Cross supplies they got. Surely that's not asking too much. After all, they are rightfully ours."

Whitey said, "There's one thing about it, we can't make them share with us, but we can sure make them wish they had."

Antagonism toward the English over the Red Cross supplies continued, and one evening, we heard a commotion at the barricade at the gate of our compound. We ran to see what was the matter. Three Englishmen were lying on the ground, beaten to a pulp. With looks of unconcern, in walked "Zip Zomo" and "Circles," who had just flattened the Englishmen.

The next morning, as usual, up came General Blackbourne and his staff. With them was the Captain, Sergeant Major and Corporal who got whipped the night before. They had us lined up in two ranks facing each other, and were going to pick out the culprits who whipped them. When they got about to the middle some wise guy on the other end said, "Who cut down the cherry tree?" Of course, everyone on our end chimed in, "George Washington!"

As we did so, we surrounded them. The General became very flustered and lost his composure. "Hear, hear," he said. "Colonel Thorpe, can't you control your men?"

"Certainly," Colonel Thorpe said. "O.K. men, fall back, make room for the General to depart."

After they had left and we enjoyed a good laugh, Colonel Thorpe had us fall in again to read us the new camp orders.

"As of today, there shall be no more trading, fighting, black marketing, stealing, pilfering, or scrounging. By Order of her Majesty's Royal Army. Signed, General Blackbourne."

"Now men," Colonel Thorpe shouted, "you heard the

orders." Then lowering his voice, "Don't get caught!"

Two nights later I was sitting on the terrace of the English football field, when someone tapped me on the shoulder and said, "Come on."

I looked up and it was Whitey. I followed him around behind the building until he stopped. Whispering to me he said, "This is the Limey police headquarters. Here, I want to show you something. See that suitcase hanging on the wall, it's full of loot. I know there is some money and jewelry in it. It belongs to that Limey Sergeant Major in charge of their M.P. force, and you know what a racketeer and shakedown artist he is."

"What are we waiting on?" I asked. "Let's get it and get the hell out of here."

"Just a minute. You see that guy through the door in there? They left him here to guard it during the show. When you see me talking to him, you raise the window. I'll take care of him, and come through this window with the suitcase."

Whitey walked calmly around to the front of the M.P. headquarters, in the door, and approached the guy at the desk as if to shoot the breeze. Then it happened. He sucker punched him, and came scrambling through the window, handing me the suitcase as he escaped. We took off through the brush, and hadn't gone far when we heard the alarm sounded and the screaming of orders for our capture.

We stopped beside a tree in a dried up creek bed. Taking a rock, I broke the lock on the suitcase and we examined our haul. There were three or four hundred pounds English money, and a few bills from other countries. The jewelry was just junk so we threw it away. There were also a couple of bars of American soap which we kept. Hiding the loot inside our pants, we headed home. As we turned a corner, we walked right into an English patrol out looking for us.

"Hi," I said. "What's all the excitement? People running up and down these roads like mad."

"Some bloke's robbed the Sergeant Major and we got them surrounded in this valley."

"Whitey," I said, "that must be the two we saw running across the road carrying something back there."

"Blimey," the M.P. said, "which way did they go?"

"Across that blacktop road and up that creek bed."

"Thanks," he said. "Forward quick march."

Whitey and I turned and headed for the barracks. Whitey said, "My God, how dumb and gullible can you get?"

10

On the Outside

I first heard about "Slade" while sitting about shooting the breeze and playing cards. He was an Australian soldier on the other side of camp who was a black marketeer and racketeer. Rumors were circulating that he had been slipping out of camp at night and dealing with the natives and Chinese.

Bright and early one morning, Whitey and I headed for the other side of the camp to look up Slade. As we approached the area where he was, the prison camp began to look like a hobo jungle. Shacks and lean-tos of all kinds had been built. We asked directions to his quarters, and I knocked on the door.

"Come in," I heard someone say.

I opened the door and peered cautiously inside. Two guys were sitting at a small wooden table, and one was piled up in a wooden bunk. Introductions were made and we were invited to join the two Aussies at the table for tea.

"Where's this guy Slade?" I asked.

"That's him up there Snowy. I'll wake him up so you Yanks can deal with him, if you like."

He shook Slade, and he rolled over to face us, stretching. He said, "Hi, Yanks! What can I do for you?" As he climbed out of the bunk, he looked like a giant to me. I stood alongside him and looked up to him and said, "Man, you're a horse. How big are you?"

"Well now, Yank, I'm six feet five and weigh sixteen stone. I'm all guts and muscle and I fear no man." Taking a small stool from under the bunk, he stood on it and put his head in a harness rigged with springs in the ceiling, and started to exercise his neck muscles. He did this for about twenty minutes, and then stepped down. "Try it, Snowy," he laughed.

"Why I can't even reach that contraption," I stammerd, "but if you'll lift me up there, I'd like to try it."

"Here," he said, "stand on this bench, then you can reach it." He placed my head in the harness and adjusted it. "Now Snowy, just put your hands on your hips, brace your legs and move your head back and forth from side to side."

"It looked real easy when I saw you do it, Slade, but I can't even move this thing, much less jar the rafters of this shack the way you did."

Whitey and I spent the rest of the morning with Slade, and through the conversation with the other Australians around the area, we found out he was much older than he looked. He had played eighteen years of professional rugby football in Australia before the war.

Slade sold us a few hundred cigars, some cigarettes, salt and slabs of brown sugar. All in all, we had quite a day with him, but we realized we must get back to our own area. We bade all our new friends goodbye except Slade. He said he'd walk a ways with us.

"Snowy," he said, "I'd like you to go outside of camp with me some night. If you want a few little thrills, I'll be glad to take you, and I'll bring you back all safe and sound in one piece. You'll really be surprised how easy it is when you have the connections. Tomorrow night is my night to make contact. If you want to go with me, and do a little trading, and buying, you come to my place tomorrow afternoon before it's too late to get through that no-man's land by ferry, from your camp to ours."

"I'd kinda like to go. I'll think it over, and if I can make it, Whitey and I will be at your place early tomorrow afternoon."

"Well, so long you Yankee bastards. I'll look for you blokes tomorrow." With this, Slade turned and headed back to his shack.

"What do you think, Whitey? Do you think it would be worth the risk to slip out of camp with him?"

"I don't know. He's been doing it and getting away with it. If you don't go, I'd sure like to go in your place. At least if we are going to try it, one of us should go with him first, to learn the ropes. There would be no use to go out there and run around like a chicken with its head off, not knowing where we were going, and maybe get shot besides. One thing for sure, he's sure big enough to protect you. Do you think you'll go?"

"I don't know yet." By this time we were at the ferry. It was just a valley and we had to wait for the flag to go across in a group. We were lying back on the side of the ditch alongside the road when the group from the other side arrived.

Someone barked, "Attention!" and when I looked up, there was as much gold braid as I'd ever seen. It was the Dutch Air Marshal General I had sold the whiskey to in Java. He came over to Whitey and me and we gave him a package of cigars. He told us the Japs were taking him to Japan, and that he and his staff were on their way to depart from Singapore now. Bidding him farewell, we wished him good luck as he was marched on down the road.

That night, neither Whitey nor I got much sleep because of our nervous anticipation of my going outside with Slade. We got to Slade's early in the afternoon and made our preparations to slip outside as soon as it was dark enough. Slade provided me with a pair of dark coveralls and a dark sock-cap. We were ready to make our departure when Slade moved the table back, brushed aside the dirt and raised a trap door. He reached down, came up with a couple of pistols, handed me one, and put the other in his belt. I must have had a frightened look because he said, "Now Snowy, don't get scared. These are just for emergency purposes only." Handing me two small Jap hand grenades he added, "Now all you have to do in case someone would get after us is unscrew the cap and drop it and run. O.K., Snowy, let's go. Stay close to me and right behind me. When you can't see me, hold onto me."

We made our way to the trees alongside the two rolls of coiled barb wire and Slade motioned for me to sit down.

We had to wait a few minutes until the Jap patrol went by. They came marching down between the barb wire and went on by. Slade said, "O.K., follow me."

The wire had been cut from his previous excursions and just hooked back together. He unhooked it and motioned for me to step through. He did the same thing at the second coil, and we were on the outside. Slade stopped, stretched, took a deep breath and said, "Boy, this outside air sure smells good. Step out, Snowy, follow me."

We went down a lane which led out into a large sweeping valley. After crossing it, we came out on a blacktop road. "My God, Slade, how far have we traveled?" I asked. "I'm getting pretty tired."

"Only about five miles so far, Snowy, but we got to make it to a bridge on down this road about another mile before we can rest."

Slade knew his way well, and turned down a side path. We approached the bridge from the side, along a small stream. "O.K., take a rest, Snowy. We have to wait here until another patrol comes over the bridge. Only this time I have to stop them to give them their payoff. But they are not Japs, they are Malay police working for the Japs."

We heard them come marching down the road and stop as they approached the bridge. I followed Slade and we met them in the middle of the bridge. Slade did all the talking, I just listened. He also gave the Malay Sergeant in charge of the patrol, one hundred dollars in Jap script money. He seemed very grateful to Slade for some reason. He thanked him and proceeded down the road with his patrol. I sure breathed a sigh of relief.

We started down the road again and Slade said, "The village is just over the rise there, Snowy. First of all, we'll see what Mama-San has cooking for us."

We came into the village from the back side and were met by an elderly Chinese man who spoke English. "Everything O.K., Mister Slade, we go to my house now. Mama-San, she cook good for you."

The Chinaman's house was near the middle of the village and set up above the ground about six feet on stilts. We climbed the stairs and sat down on the straw mats on the floor. Mama-San came in from the back with steaming hot rice and a lovely rich pork stew, which she gave us in small round dishes. It really tasted good, but Slade warned me not to eat too much because it was too rich and would make me sick. While we were sipping our tea, Slade said,

"Snowy, relax. The Japs don't ever even come this way. O.K., Pappa-San, run in your salesmen. We're ready to buy if you got anything of value." He left and Slade said to me, "Don't be in a hurry to buy anything from these guys until after we dicker with them a couple of hours."

Pappa-San brought his boys in one at a time, to let Slade and me look at their stuff. After two or three hours of dickering with them, I ended up with a packful of cigars, tobacco, sugar and salt. I figured that's the only thing they had which would be of any value if I got it back inside camp. Slade said we better be getting started back to camp because we had to be there before it started getting light tomorrow morning.

We retraced our steps back to camp and arrived safely at the wire. Slade made a check up and down the wire and said, "O.K., Snowy, the coast is clear, let's go." As we slipped through that last coil of barbed wire, I breathed a sigh of relief.

When we arrived back at Slade's shack, Whitey stepped out and said, "Jesus, I thought you guys would never get back. How'd you make out? Did you do any good?"

"Yeah," I said, "I got a packful of junk here. Split it up half for you and half for me, to carry back to our own camp in the morning. In the meantime, let's get some sleep and rest."

11

"Who's in Charge Here?"

We arrived back at our own compound the next morning in time to fall in for our morning muster, and were detailed to go on a working party, our first to Singapore. Captain Parker who was in charge of our detail, marched us down to the prison tool house. When we got there and were waiting to draw our tools to go to work, Captain Parker turned to a corporal, "Zip" Zumo who was with us and said, "Take charge, Zip."

Zip said, "O.K., you guys fall out alongside the road in the shade and smoke. No use to stand in this hot sun." While we were lounging alongside the road, an English Major strutted up and told us to fall in. We just laughed, and a few of the guys gave him the raspberries.

"I say there," he said, "who's in charge here?"

Zip got up, ambled over to him and said, "I am. Why?"

"Well, I am Major so-and-so of his Majesty's Royal Army,

and I'm telling you to fall these men in at attention."

"Well now, isn't that interesting," Zip said. "I'm Corporal Zumo of Texas." Then, Bam! The Major never knew what hit him. Two or three Englishmen came and carried him away.

Captain Parker came back to see what all the commotion was, and two or three English officers stepped up to tell him to arrest Zip for assaulting their Major. Captain Parker said, "Zip, front and center."

Zip went up front and Captain Parker proceeded to tell him,

"Zip, you know better than that, so you just go back to the barracks. You've done your day's work for today."

We all laughed while the Englishmen just shook their heads, dumbfounded, and walked away.

We spent the rest of that day helping cut down rubber trees and leveling off the ground to build an airport. After getting back to our barracks that night, I was just lying around on my bed resting, when up walked Whitey.

"Hey Nick, guess what I found - a whole briefcase full of money!"

"Where is it?" I asked.

"Oh, I haven't got it yet. I'll need your help. It will take two of us to get it."

"O.K., let's go," I said as I got up off the bed.

We started down the road toward the Dutch officer's quarters. "Hey," I said, "are you sure we are going in the right direction, Whitey?"

"Yes, I been casing this job for a long time. It will be just like taking candy from a baby. When we get there, you stand watch on the veranda and I'll get the loot. This old boy keeps his briefcase hanging up behind the door and a mosquito net tied to it. Now if he wakes up, we'll have to get out of there fast."

"I don't know, Whitey. That moon's pretty bright tonight. If someone gets after us, they will be pretty hard to shake off tonight."

"I'll tell you," he said, "if anyone gets after us, we'll run through one of those English barracks and let them get the blame for it. O.K.?"

By this time we were on the veranda of the building we were looking for. I stood beside the door and Whitey stepped inside. I heard the string holding the mosquito net snap. I peeped in and saw the net fall. Out came Whitey with the briefcase. Quietly we walked off the veranda and down the road.

Whitey said, "Take it easy. We got plenty of time. That guy didn't even wake up. I know there's money in this thing, because I sold that guy some cigars and he took the money out of here to pay me."

"Listen, Whitey, just in case there might be something real valuable in here, let's get rid of the evidence so no one will ever know besides us." We went up on top of a small hill in the moonlight, cut around the back of the briefcase and opened it. It contained money, jewelry, and papers. We took the money and jewelry and burned the papers. The briefcase we threw down a toilet hole and shoved dirt in on top of it. We got back to our own area without any trouble and went to bed.

The next day the rumors were flying hot and heavy about the Dutchman's briefcase and his great loss. To Whitey and me it was really a farce because we actually knew what was missing in that briefcase.

12

The Boxing Meet

Whitey and I laid low until the episode of the briefcase cooled off and confined our activities to our own compound. I was engrossed in a poker game this particular afternoon when Whitey said,

"Hey look, a Limey delegation. I wonder what those chipper so-and-so's want?"

"I don't know, but we'll soon find out. Let's see what they have to say."

Gathering up our chips and money, we met the Limey delegation by the corner of the barracks. They seemed to be led by an old time boxer who was manager of their boxing team.

"Hi, Yanks," he said. "We are here to offer you a challenge by our boxing team for a show one week from this Sunday. We'll wait for your answer."

We retreated to the veranda to talk the situation over

among ourselves and decide whether or not we'd take them on. Our boxers, of which we had many, readily agreed. I guess they thought they could release all the hates they had built up against the English in the ring.

Zip Zumo spoke up. "O.K. Nick, go tell them we'll be ready for all twelve bouts. You be our manager."

"Me?" I said. "I don't know enough about boxing to manage you guys."

"You don't have to know anything. We'll do the boxing. Just tell them we'll be there."

I went back out to the Limeys and said, "We'll be there - whereabouts and what time?"

"Bloody good, Yank. As I say, one week from Sunday at one o'clock on the football field in the valley. We'll have the ring set up and we'll go three rounds. O.K.?"

"Yeah, O.K., we'll see you." Turning to Zip I said, "My gosh, you think we can whip those guys?"

"Whip 'em - we'll clobber 'em!"

"What makes you so sure?"

"Well, let's see, we got fifteen or twenty real good boxers among our army personnel, and there's a few good ones among you sailors. Don't worry, we'll take care of those guys."

As the day of our boxing show approached, I grew steadily more anxious. Whenever I checked up on the English boxing team, they were doing road work, skipping rope, shadow boxing and sparring about all day long. I'd go back to our barracks and here'd be our guys, sitting around shooting the breeze or playing poker if they weren't working. If I said anything to them, they'd cut me short and say, "Go mind your own business!"

Finally the day of reckoning came, and we showed up. I'll never forget the death-like hush that fell over the Limey cheering section about midway through the bouts. It was time for their best boxer to meet Snake, our American-Indian boxer who had been Oklahoma State Golden Gloves champion. As a child he had been kicked in the face by a horse and a jagged scar ran down through the middle of his nose and cheek.

In all the years he had boxed, he had never been beaten. A finer person I have never met than Snake. I was working in his corner as he prepared to take on the best of the British.

The first round Snake went out and never threw a punch. When the bell rang and he returned to the corner I said, "My gosh, Snake, what's the matter?"

"Take it easy, boy, I'm just feeling him out. I'll drop him quick this round."

The ten-second whistle sounded, and the Limey fans were still going wild. As the bell sounded, Snake went out to meet his opponent. He faked a left jab and followed through with a beautiful right cross. The Limey went down like someone hit him with a sledge hammer. I remember remarking, "That's the only time I ever saw anyone win a fight by only throwing one punch."

In all, I guess we really had a glorious day. Out of twelve fights we won eleven by knockouts, and the other by a T.K.O.

13

"Pray for Me"

As usual, the Japs loaded us into the small metal box-cars like animals. I was lucky, I thought; they didn't lock the doors - just placed a couple of guards on each side of the car in the doorways. In our uncomfortable positions, time on our trip up the Malayan Peninsula seemed endless. At one particular mountain pass, the stench was unbearable. When the Japs made their surge down the coast, the Scottish highlanders had set up defense positions in this mountain pass, and there were still piles of dead Japs on each side of the railroad.

Singapore will always hold fond memories for me, I guess, but it also built up my hate and disgust for the English to the extent that I'm afraid I'll never have any respect for them at all. Just the opposite was true for the Australians, Scotch, Irish, Dutch, and other nationalities. I'll never forget the beaming look on the Scotch bagpipe players face as he piped us from the camp as we marched out of camp to the railroad station to leave Singapore.

As the sun rose for the second time in the doorway of our dank steam infested cars, we arrived at the end of the line, and at our destination in the city of Pedang. Before we even had a chance to stretch our legs and get the kinks out of them, the Japs had us headed through the bomb-torn yards and docks alongside a Jap ship which was awaiting our arrival. It was an exact replica of all the others I'd seen, and just as filthy and dirty.

We were quartered in the forward hold on the main deck, just in front of the ship's bridge. As usual, bunks were made of rough lumber and were four shelves high. Toilet facilities were a couple of buckets out in the middle of the deck. In case of an emergency, our only means of escape was up a small wooden ladder tied to the side of the hatch combing.

At least they did feed us. Our first good meal came soon after we were settled down aboard ship. They lowered wooden buckets of hot steaming curried rice down to us and a bucket of slimy cooked seaweed that had a fishy taste. With a full stomach, I lay back and went to sleep. When I awoke that evening, I found that the Japs were letting us go topside to get a little air and sunshine.

On climbing up the ladder to topside, I was met with a heavenly sea breeze. Even though the setting sun was hot, the breeze was cooling. Also, I discovered we were no longer alone. After leaving the Straits of Malacca and heading north into the Bay of Bengal, we had been joined by four other transports with four destroyers as escorts.

The following day, I was standing on the port side of the ship watching the destroyers and other ships, and just looking at the sea. Someone tapped me on the shoulder, and

I looked around to find a small Jap alongside me. He was very young and childish looking. I thought surely he must be some crew member's son. To my amazement I discovered he was a Zero pilot, a college graduate and a volunteer into the Air Force. He came from a well-to-do family in Japan. Therefore he drew no salary; his folks paid him directly by mail. I had quite a time with him for the next couple of days; he gave me his cigarettes, matches, soap, and a supply of tooth powder and a tooth brush. I never found out what power he had over the other Japs, but anything I asked him for that he didn't have, he would make the other pilots fork over.

Our ship could only make about five knots, so our convoy traveled pretty slowly. The third day out, I was lying on top of the hatch cover just looking up at the clouds floating by overhead, when suddenly, like a large hovering vulture, an American four engine bomber swooped down upon us from astern. He flew straight on by and started his bombing run on the lead ships in the convoy. I jumped to my feet and raced to the life line for a better view. I then realized that there were four of the large planes, making pattern runs from all directions at the congested convoy. Suddenly the whole world seemed to erupt. Ships blew up all around us and the water began to be covered with debris of the sinking ships.

One of my buddies, "Hiet", was standing alongside me, and I said, "Well, it won't be long now - here comes one at us." We took cover under a steel ladder that led up to the bridge of the ship on the starboard side. When the action started, I immediately began to pray as usual. Suddenly Hiet grabbed me by the arm and said, "Pray for me!"

It had happened before, so I kind of expected it. I looked at him, terror stricken, and thanked God that I knew how to pray. It always seemed to me the most horrible thing in the world to see Hiet in this condition. He seemed to die a dozen agonizing deaths, and looked as if he were going to explode with fear.

"Let's see if we can get up this ladder to the wing of the super structure. If their bombs hit, they will go below before exploding, and we'd have a better chance to leave this tub."

"O.K.," Hiet said. "Lead the way."

I swung around on the hand rail and started up, but I was stopped cold by the machine gun the Japs had set up at the top of the ladder and the Jap guards with their fixed bayonets. It was too late to try to do anything else, so we dove under the ladder for cover.

Everything seemed to be happening at once. I clung to the steel deck for dear life, even though I couldn't tell whether I was up or down. Near misses on each side of us made me feel as if the bombs were landing in our lap. The Japs at the top of the ladder were all dead-cut down by shrapnel from the bombs. Their blood poured down on me, making me feel clammy and sticky wet. I thanked God they hadn't let us up the ladder.

The Jap Captain now stood holding onto the forward rail of the bridge with a bloody battle dressing over his right eye. A stack of small caliber ammunition on the fantail was on fire, and bullets were pinging in every direction. A Jap sailor alongside me was struggling with a fire hose and motioned for me to help him. I grabbed the hose and went aft through the Jap pilot's quarters on the port side toward the fire. The expressions on their faces was killing. They had their life jackets on, all ready to abandon ship. Some of them already had.

An Australian sailor from the HMS Perth connected the hose and I played it on the fire from behind a gun cut shield. Alongside me knelt the Jap sailor and the Australian. All the other Japs had fled the area. The Jap kept telling us how brave we were to be fighting the fire for him. He kept wanting to look at the fire over the gun shield and finally after the bullets began to quiet down, I lost patience with him and I said, "O.K., go ahead and look!"

He raised his head above the gun shield and as he did so, I heard a dull splat. A bullet had hit him between the eyes, then he just crumpled to the deck. I started to roll him for his money or anything else of value he might have on him, then stopped and looked around to see if any Japs were watching. By the time I turned back, the Aussie was already shoving him under the life-line.

"Don't worry, Snowy," he said, "I got his watch and money. We'll split fifty-fifty."

We got the fire out, and I discovered some of the blood on my leg was my own. At first I thought it was a bullet sticking under the side of my knee cap, but upon closer examination I discovered it was a piece of shrapnel. I limped back forward to where the other prisoners had been. Some of them had been killed, but I found "Copp," our first aid man, down in the hole yet, so I climbed down to see what he could do for my leg. I had to sit down on the deck and wait my turn - he was busy!

Arriving to me he said, "Well now, let me get my forceps. I'll fix you right up, Nick."

"You don't mean those old rusty things you pull teeth with do you?" I asked apprehensively.

"Yep, them's the ones," he said as he came up out of his bag of gear.

I looked the other way as he pulled and tugged at the shrapnel protruding from my leg. When it finally broke loose, it felt like he had pulled my whole insides out.

"Here's a souvenir," he said. "Keep it; maybe it will bring you luck. Wrap that leg up now until that hole heals. There may be a few flakes left in there, but they'll be o.k. if you don't get an infection in your leg."

We picked up survivors from the other ships in the convoy, and crowded them aboard our ship. As I stood looking over the side, an incredible spectacle unfolded before my eyes. Concussion from exploding bombs had killed a large number of fish, and in spite of the fact that their lives were in danger, the survivors couldn't resist the temptation of a seafood feast. Many of them were swimming with one hand while dragging dead fish in the other. One Dutchman outdid them all; he appeared alongside with a fish in each hand and a little baby kitten perched on his head. He was having quite a struggle trying to make it up the side of the cargo net, so a couple of us leaned down and pulled him up. The poor little cat's tail had been blown off, so we bandaged him up as best we could. He looked like a wet, sick rat. We all formed an immediate sentimental attachment to him, so we decided to keep him as our mascot. We held a vote on various names to call him, and finally decided on "Shipwreck."

About sun-up the next morning, we made port at Moulmein, Burma. The Japs herded us from the ship like cattle and marched us past a primitive shipyards where wooden ships were being built, mostly by hand, with the aid of work elephants.

"What a delightful and educational experience for the children of the world!" I thought. "If only they all could see these elephants lifting heavy timbers, putting them in place, and driving in the wooden pegs with large wooden mallets held in their trunks.

We were prodded onward until we came alongside the prison wall. As we turned into the open gate, the stale, rancid odor of the unwashed, dysentery-ridden occupants who had preceded us nearly slapped me down. But in spite of this first impression, things went pretty smoothly in the Moulmein Prison. Compared to other places where I had been confined, I actually enjoyed my stay here, except for the unusual abuse from the guards. At least they gave us enough rice to prevent that incessant gnawing feeling inside from chronic hunger, and the weather was wonderful.

That first night I was amazed when the moon suddenly loomed up over the prison wall. It seemed so big and so near that I got a feeling that I could just reach up and touch it. I remember thinking.

I don't know who wrote "Moon Over Burma", but he sure knew what he was talking about."

The Japs didn't lock us in cells, but gave us the freedom of the compound. This seemed strange to me, until

I realized that there was no room for us in the already over-crowded cells. So we bedded down along the inside of the prison walls.

Taking a tattered Bible from the bottom of my boot bag, I read the Twenty-First Psalm by the moonlight before going to sleep.

14

The Death Railroad

The next morning I was on a working party for the Japs. They loaded ten of us in a truck and drove to a large pagoda.

"I wonder if this is the same one Kipling wrote about?" I asked Bull.

"If it is," he said, "he was off his rocker, because it sure doesn't face eastward across the sea."

The Japs had been looting the pagoda of all its precious and semi-precious stones, even going so far as chipping small pieces of jade from the pillars inside. Looking at the helpless Burmese, I realized they must be thinking as I; if the Japs were building Asia for the Asiatics, it must be all one way for the Japs.

We hauled the crates of loot to the docks and loaded them aboard a ship. I never did find out whether the officer in charge was shipping the loot to Japan for the government or for himself. But from the way he acted with the captain of the ship, I suspected it was about a fifty-fifty deal.

Well, I knew of one piece of jade that, with good luck, would never get to Japan. I had put it in my G-string while loading the truck. At the time I took it, I didn't even know it was jade or its true value. But while I was a prisoner, I never passed up anything I thought would be of any value and could be traded to the natives for something to eat.

On the fifth day I was again nabbed for a working party. Had I known what was coming in the next few hours, I sure would have tried to finagle my way out of it. As always, I was prepared to take a lot of guff from the guards. Instead, they were very apologetic when we discovered we were to bury our own dead from the ships. The truck stopped alongside the corpses in the hot sun on the dock. The stench was practically unbearable until you got used to it. The first five bodies we loaded into the truck without any trouble, but the remaining three we had to shovel into the back of the truck.

Completing the loading, we climbed aboard and went across the town to a small cemetery, beautifully located by a small church on the edge of a woods. The Jap guards laid out an area about six feet square and told us to dig one large grave for all the bodies.

I was standing about knee deep in the grave when my attention was called to the church about fifty yards away. Standing alongside it were two Catholic sisters dressed in complete habit. I waved to them and they returned the greeting. I kept one eye on them and one on the Jap guard nearby. It wasn't long until one of the Sisters motioned for

The Death Railroad

me to come over to the church.

Getting the guard's permission to go to the toilet, I ambled back through the trees toward the side of the church. I stopped behind a large tree out of sight of the guards and called softly to the Sisters. Unmindful of the fates that might befall them, they hastily walked over to me.

"Hello," they said. "Who are you and where do you come from?"

"I'm just an American sailor who was captured in Java and brought here by the Japs to work on the Burma railroad. Just one of the mass, I guess."

One of the Sisters motioned to the other and she said, "He must be hungry. Bring him some food."

"Keep it for yourself, Sister, I'll get along O.K."

"No, you don't understand; we have plenty and we want to share it with you. After all, that's why we are here, to help in any way we can, not only spiritually. How have the Japs been treating you?"

"As good as can be expected, I guess. About the same as they treat their own soldiers."

The other Sisters returned with a small tray containing a cup of tea, rice, meat stew, and three small cookies. The aroma was overwhelming. I sat down behind the tree and gulped it all down like a starved animal. The Sisters had moved back from me and I realized it must be the pungent odor of death that I carried with me.

"How pale they look with their white skin," I thought. "They even look sick and underfed themselves, and yet here they share their food with me. I guess the good Lord does look after his own. They don't act as if they have a care or worry in the world."

After I returned to the work detail, it didn't take long to finish filling the grave. Someone said a few words of prayer, and we climbed back into the truck to return to prison. On the way back the Japs stopped by a small bridge and let us go down a small creek and take a bath. It was sure refreshing to leave some of the stink and smell behind.

The first words I heard upon our arrival back in prison were from Bull who said, "Pack your gear, we are moving out tomorrow morning."

"Where are we going?" I asked.

"Into the jungle to work on the railroad, I guess. That's what we came here for."

Early the next morning the Japs herded us into the trucks for our trip to the first camp in the Burma jungle. The trip was hot, dirty, and so dusty that everyone had a rag of some kind tied over his nose and mouth to keep out the dust. After about six hours of hectic thrills with the wild driving Japs, we arrived at our work camp.

It was just a bunch of bamboo huts with Adapt leaf roofs, set in a clearing alongside the dirt railroad bed. At the gate was a lean-to type Jap guardhouse and light guards on duty. A fence of bamboo circled the entire camp.

We were marched inside and assigned the first barracks to our left. There was no flooring inside, but on each side were ramp-like projections to sleep on. Each of us was assigned a space about two-and-one-half feet wide to make our bunks on.

The Death Railroad

No sooner had I settled down and got stretched out than I heard the Japs yelling "Tinko", or fall in. They divided us into details or "Kamies" of twenty-five people for work the next day. After falling out, we began to play cards and take inventory of our new surroundings.

In the camp with us were Dutch, English, Australian, and just across the back fence were about five thousand Tamils from India, known in the Orient as the "Gypsies." The camp was hot and dirty so no one wore clothes other than just a G-string.

The Jap officer in charge briefed our officers on what was expected of us while we were here. He told them that engineers of the English and American Government had surveyed this railroad in 1935, but had given up building it because it would cost too much in equipment and loss of lives. But these were minor details as far as the Japs were concerned; we were going to build it strictly with man power.

I found out what he meant, because when the sun rose the next morning, we were already working with those picks and shovels. The Jap guards in charge of my detail measured off the quota of dirt we were supposed to move onto a fill in the railroad bed. It totaled out to two square meters per man. They let us know that our work day wouldn't finish until the job was completed. To carry the dirt up on the rail bed, we had yo-ho poles on which we had a rice sack fastened to each corner by wire. Two men carrying one of these things can move an awful lot of dirt in one day. My first day was rather uneventful. The job was finished about four-thirty and the guards marched us back to camp. I was so tired that I sacked out immediately after eating my rice. The split bamboo poles I slept on felt like a mattress.

The following day while digging down in the hole with a shovel, I struck the root of a stump. When I reached down to remove it, I received a vicious sting on my hand by a small scorpion. In no time at all I was feverish and had a large knot under my arm. For the next few days I was quite ill. At least the experience made me aware of the real dangers that lurk in the jungle. I was going to have to be more careful if I was going to survive.

Finally the Japs gave us a day off to rest and catch up on our laundry and camp work. Sometimes I thought it would be better if we were kept busy instead of being given a chance to loaf and get into trouble with the camp guards or other prisoners. On this particular day, Zip who had been working as a mess attendant for the Japs, came walking through the hut and a boy named Russel who was sitting down at the foot of the bunks gave the command:

"Kee-out-ski" (Attention!) It was meant as an insult and was usually saved for Jap guards at the head of the list. Before anyone knew what happened, Zip took a couple of steps, turned and hit him across the eyes and nose. Russ slumped to the floor bleeding like a stuck hog, and Zip just turned and walked out.

Snake was sitting on my bunk shooting the breeze about Oklahoma when it happened, and looking at me with fire shooting from his eyes he said, "I sure wish that S.O.B. would try that on me."

"Yeah," I said, "and remember what the doctor said, we have to be careful about hitting anybody because now since we been eating this rice so long, our bones are soft and we might injure someone seriously."

The next time I saw Russell was about three days later, and was he a mess. The doctor had a couple of pieces of rubber hose running from his nose, and you could hardly tell where his eyes were. I noticed at this time for some reason I didn't feel sorry for him. It seemed I had gotten to the point where I had no emotions, just feelings of depression. It wasn't just me though, it was all the P.O.W.'s because of when we were first captured and saw someone being tortured or injured, we'd get mad and feel sorry for them. But now, even when the Japs were beating on someone we'd just look and say, "I wonder what that stupid so and so did to get the Japs on him this time." Thank God I still had a sense of humor, because I really think it kept me going. Many times I laughed during serious situations, and it seemed to get rid of all those pent-up emotions and make life just a little more bearable.

The following day I was assigned to a new work detail. Our task was to make a large cut through the side of a hill for the railroad bed. The officer in charge of our detail was a shady character we knew very little about. Just before the capitulation of Java, Colonel Thorpe, who was senior officer of the American forces, received a phone call to pick up an American from the docks in Batavia. When he arrived at the docks, he was met by a Dutch sea captain who told him he had the person he was to pick up locked up in the brig. Not because of anything he had done, but by his request for his own protection. It seemed he was worried because he had two suitcases full of American money and was afraid someone would kill him for it or rob him of it.

Never did he give a satisfactory explanation of who he was, where he came from, or where he got all the money. Speculation and rumors were that he'd deserted from the Phillipines with a payroll belonging to the Army or the Air Force. He gave his rank as Major and we accepted him as Major Macy of the U.S. Army.

After being confined for a few months, it's awfully hard to keep anything from your fellow inmates because for want of conversation, you just tell all. But never did Major Macy ever reveal anything personal about himself other than he played professional football back home in the States, and from the way he was built, I believed him.

We hadn't been working but a couple of hours when a little old Jap guard standing up on a pile of dirt accidently discharged his rifle. The bullet went through a couple of guys' legs and ricocheted off a shovel. I gasped in amazement as Major Macy rushed up to the guard, grabbed his rifle and bayonet, turned him around roughly toward camp, and booted him in the rear end. Turning to us he said, "You men keep working, I'm going to take this little slant-eyed so-and-so back to camp and make them send out a responsible guard with us. It would be bad enough to get shot without having some rube like this do it just because he can't handle a rifle."

As I watched him herd the Jap back down the railroad, I turned to Bull and said, "It sure took a lot of guts to collar that Jap guard like that."

"Yeah, I know, but what gets me is all these other guards just stood around and let him get away with it. If anyone else had tried it, as bad as we all wanted to, we'd probably get shot on the spot."

Well, Bull's prediction proved to be accurate. Major Macy became another atrocity to the Japs. When I turned by the guardhouse that night, the first thing I saw was his hands tied behind his back and lashed to his ankles. He was a mass of lumps, whelps and dried blood. About a week later when they turned him loose he was just a shadow and incoherent, couldn't hear or anything. He was in such bad shape that when we moved on, we left him behind. That was the last I ever saw of him.

15

Hooper's Funeral

The next day a Jap truck pulled up to the guardhouse with an Australian officer in the back under heavy armed guard. Undoubtedly he was the one who had escaped camp No. 75 before our arrival here. The Jap officer in charge of the camp came out in front of the guardhouse and read his orders to execute the prisoner at sun up. He also told the guards to give him anything he wanted before morning.

The first thing they did was march him over to the hospital, for our doctors to dress his wounded shoulder. Two slugs had torn through the fleshy part of his shoulder and the doctor said gangrene had already set in. He spoke his first words refusing any medication other than clean bandages.

"Save your medicine Doc. If I don't die before morning, I'll die anyway, and you'll need all the medicine you got for your own boys in this jungle."

Sometimes it's awful hard to figure out the Japs. I couldn't understand their attitude toward the condemned man. Whether it was for our benefit or to relieve the guilt from their own consciences, at least they were treating him like a human being but also exploiting his escape and recapture to the utmost.

Sleep this night was practically nil because of the silent prayers in anticipation of the early morning execution. The sun loomed up hot in a clear sky and someone remarked,

"What a beautiful day for an execution!"

Considering the conditions, I guess the Japs carried off the execution as well as could be expected. The cemetery was just across the road and they even had a truck just to haul the prisoner that far. His grave was already dug for him and the Japs had an eight man firing squad awaiting him. From where I was standing I could see the Jap officer in charge ask him if he had any last wish and he motioned for a cigarette. The Japs handed him a cigarette, lighted it for him and let him sit down on a stump to smoke it. How he did it I don't know, but he sat there just as calm as could be, leisurely smoking like he didn't have a worry in the world.

When he finished his smoke, the Japs wanted to tie his hands behind his back, blindfold him, and place him on his knees at the end of the gave. He refused, telling them he was a soldier and wanted to die like one. Striding back to the end of the grave, he stood at attention and said, "O.K., I'm ready."

The Jap officer in charge nervously gave the command to fire. The rifles cracked and the poor Aussie slumped to his knees and slid slowly back in the grave.

I felt sick, but no more so than everyone else, I guess that witnessed the execution. The Jap in charge was really shook up. He came stumbling back across the road mumbling to himself, "Tok-Song Bravo", which meant: "a lot brave." He proceeded to go on a rip roaring drunk which lasted three days. During the CO's drunk, our guards got real lax and we didn't do anything but march out to work and loaf around.

But all good must soon end; an announcement was made that the Americans would all move on into the jungle to another work camp.

The next morning, we all started out in good shape, but after a few hours of marching we were straggled all up and down the road trudging along in single file. I lagged behind with the sick and crippled in order to stay with Tony, who was sick with dysentery. The going wasn't quite as rough and hurried, and we were always looking for an easy way out.

I guess the monsoon season had started because the road was like a hog wallow. The Jap officer in charge of us had a bicycle, but because of the mud, he spent all his time pushing it through the mud holes. Some places in the road were so deep in mud you couldn't walk through them, so we found ourselves tip-toeing around the edges of the deep spots. As we passed three or four more work camps I began to realize the terrific number of prisoners the Japs must have in here to build this railway.

We had about three more miles to go yet when I looked down over a cliff into the valley below and saw some empty bull carts and four or five bulls standing around. It wasn't hard to figure out what happened. When a member of a native caravan got a case of cholera, the rest of them just ran away and left him.

I pointed them out to the Jap officer in charge and said, "Joto Muckin."

"Joto," he replied. "Muckin Mo-cho-goy."

"You mean you want me to go try and catch one?"

"All O.K.," he said.

Tony and I took off over the side of the hill toward the bulls, knowing that if we could catch one, we'd have some meat stew when we reached our new camp. They weren't hard to catch once we got to them, so when we rejoined the Jap officer at the end of the straggling line of prisoners, we each led a Burma bull.

It didn't take long to reach Camp No. 85. We just went around a hillside, made a right turn from the side of the hill, and there lay the camp. It consisted of about ten huts in all, and one large cook shack.

My life in this camp was rather uneventful other than gorging myself on stew from the two bulls Tony and I had dragged in. I was always hungry after working in the nearby railroad cuttings. Also, I always seemed to be damp and wet from the incessant rainfall.

Tony and I made our discovery here that we could fake illness on sick call and I guess I was one of the biggest bludgers the Japs ever had. It wasn't long until I had bribed my way onto a woodcutting detail and spent a lot of time hauling wood into camp and loafing around the galley.

It was on such a rainy day when a caravan of Jap supply trucks came into camp to deliver our usual supply of rations. At this time because of the bad roads and weather, they allotted us four hundred grams of rice per day. As ridiculous as it sounds, they also had a couple of loads of red pinto beans. As they progressed through the jungle, they were giving two bags to each kitchen.

"Itch", who was by now our number one cook said, "Holy mackerel, look at them beans. You guys just play it cool and I'll show you how to talk these yellow so-and-sos out of them." He casually walked over to the Jap in charge of supplies and stated, "Beans Joeto Nye. Will you please keep those damn beans and give us some more rice?"

With this, the Japs became furious and said, "No, no, no more rice. Rice for Nippon, Americano get all beans now." He proceeded to have us load the rice back on the trucks, and everytime we pushed a bag back on the truck, we'd moan and complain about losing our rice ration, and he'd have the Japs toss off another bag of beans. The more he had tossed off, the sicker we acted, until we had about twenty or twenty-five bags in exchange for our rice.

"Now," he said, "Americano lots of beans, rice-o no." The Japs all joined him in roaring laughter. We continued to put on our act, even though I was almost choking in my effort to suppress my own laughter until the Japs left. As the trucks turned down the road by our guardhouse, everyone was jubilant. I looked at Itch. He looked as if he had just won a major battle.

"Well Itch, you just won the victory of the beans," I said.

"Yeah, see how easy it is to outsmart those bastards, and they think they can win a war from us."

Itch took the remainder of the last bull and diced it up to cook with the beans, and that evening when the working parties got into camp for chow, we all ate until we were sick. Of course we all thought we were dying that night when we were racing back and forth from the toilet areas, but I figured it was worth the trips even if the food was too rich for my stomach to hold.

My stay in Camp No. 85 didn't last long, but I was there long enough to see the great devastation the jungle can do to the human body in a short time with its invisible weapons: dysentery, beri-beri, cholera, malaria, and starvation.

No one will ever believe that we had people walking around here weighing as little as thirty-nine pounds, but after a few months of starvation diet, the body begins to absorb the calcium from the bones, and they get very soft and light. Take away the body fats and liquids and you don't have much left but a mummified looking skeleton covered with wrinkled skin. A lot of fellows' teeth just fell out from the lack of vitamins, and their eyes assumed that blank stare look, like they were suffering from shock. Even those of us who were in pretty good shape had a bloated look, which is not normal.

I was packing my loot to move up to the next work camp when someone screamed "Tinko," so I fell in outside with the others. Arriving at the parade ground I saw a bunch of Jap first aid men in white coats jabbering around a table. It seemed a Dutchman on the other side of camp had broken out with what they thought was smallpox, so they were going to vaccinate us all in order to prevent an epidemic. Their procedure was quite simple; the Jap medic dipped a scalpel in pox serum and made five cuts on our shoulder forming a diamond.

I thought, "My gosh, if these all take, my arm will rot off."

So, haunted by this new fear, I slipped to the back of camp to a small stream and scrubbed the serum out with wet sand. The next day after work it was almost the same routine, except this time they sliced our ear lobes for a blood smear test. I couldn't understand their reasoning in giving us all the tests; they never gave us any medicine or vitamins to help us regain our strength. I finally decided they must consider us expendable and as long as we were able to work for them, our condition didn't matter; but if we got down seriously ill, they'd just let us die. Even if they had the medicine and supplies to properly care for our ills, I doubt very much if they would have taken care of our sick people.

Death became a common and accepted occurrence at this point. All of us who escaped it walked around in a waking coma. We seemed to have no feelings or control over our actions. After you've drifted into this state of confusion, there seemed to be no hope. But I was one of the lucky ones I guess; whether it was from my constant prayers and belief in God, or the shock of Hooper's funeral service, I'll never know, but I seemed to come to my senses at Hoop's funeral.

I was on the grave digging detail the morning they carried his corpse up for burial. Walking behind it was Hooper's diminutive friend we called "Bulldog". They were really the extreme opposites. Hooper was a large bulk of a man, and "Bulldog" a small muscular build. Hooper claimed to be a former professional wrestler from Chicago, and "Bulldog" was a former Navy boxer from my ship.

We set the corpse into the shallow grave and covered the nude form with a grass mat. We never buried anyone with clothing of any kind because of the value of the cloth. Bandy was there to blow his taps on his old beat-up horn. Handing me a tattered Bible he said, "Okay, Nick, read the Scripture."

Clutching the Bible between my hands I recited the Twenty-third Psalm as if in a trance. As the eerie sounds of the bugle died away in the distant hills of the jungle, I was awakened from my trance-like state by Bandy removing it from my hands.

"O.K.," I said, "let's cover him up."

"Wait a minute," someone said. I looked around and it was "Bulldog" making his way through the mud to the head of the grave. He didn't say anything, just leaned over, removed the straw mat from Hooper's face, and deliberately spat into it.

"What's that for?" I asked.

"Oh, I don't know, I just always wanted to spit in that big so-and-so's face!"

"My God!" I thought. "What kind of animals are we becoming? If this keeps up we'll all go insane or die." Right then and there I made a vow in my silent prayers to God that I'd try, no matter what the hardships were, to live a rich full life and always conduct myself in a gentlemanly manner.

16

Camp No. 100

It seemed as though every move in the jungle became harder, as I trudged through the mud on sore feet, battling the usual flies and insects of the jungle. As I staggered by the guardhouse I thought,

"My gosh, if it had been another mile I don't believe I'd have made it." Of course, I was carrying a lot of excess junk I should have dumped along the way, but everything here had value, and there was always a chance I might trade some of it to the natives for something to eat. "So this is Camp No. 100," I mused, to no one in particular. "I wonder how many we'll leave buried on the hillside when we move on from here?"

Not long after my arrival here I got hold of a small silver cigarette case that the Jap Sergeant of the guards wanted to buy. I stalled him off for a few days, hoping I could trade it for some medicine. He didn't say much, just looked at me, and I tried to stay clear of him until I cooled off a little bit. Everything went fine until a few days later when I was on a detail to help haul water to the kitchen with a Jap truck.

During the course of the day we made about twelve trips by the guardhouse with the truck. The driver was a little buck-toothed Jap, who must have been a rick-shaw coolie before the war. On one trip by the guardhouse, which sat on a hill, I was helping shift gears to keep the truck from rolling back into our kitchen; I didn't salute the guards or the sergeant. Another prisoner in the back of the truck didn't either.

Needless to say, the sadistical little guard was waiting for us when we returned to camp that night. I could tell by the gleam in his eyes, he was happy to have the excuse to get on me. He stood the two of us at attention in front of the guardhouse and broke out the rawhide whip. It had been made by hanging the penis of a bull in a tree in the hot tropic sun and tying a weight to it so it would stretch.

After strutting around us like a banty rooster, and waving the whip like a raving monster, he raised it above his head in two hands behind me. I braced myself and tried to show no signs of fear, as experience had taught me it would only make the situation worse. Lightning flashed, blue stars streaked before my eyes and I felt warm blood oozing down my back.

The last I remembered the eight guards were taking turns on us with the whip. When I came to, I was lying on my stomach in my bunking space, a mass of dried blood and dirt, too sore to move. When I began to move around I was surprised to find out it had been two days since I received my beating. But I thanked God I had survived the ordeal at all; the other poor guy never did wake up.

There's an old proverbial phrase, "Every dog has his day." I had mine with the sergeant some days later after I recuperated from my beating. I'd been working on the rock pile in the quarry. The job sounded simple; make little rock out of big ones for use as ballast on the railway bed. Every day we'd have to crack anywhere from two to four square meters of rock per day, all according to the whims of the Jap in charge. That meant you had to stack the rock in a nice neat pile so it could be measured at the end of the working day. Of course, the day didn't end until everyone had broken his quota of stone. The inside of all my stacks were filled with stumps, logs, leaves or anything else I could slip in when the guards weren't looking. Luckily I bribed my way into doing the drilling of the blasting holes in the rock facing for the Jap powder monkey in charge of the rock quarry. Four of us were on the detail, and each two of us only had to drill four holes per day to complete our day's work.

After we'd finished our drilling on this particular day, I was sitting on a rock pile in the shade talking to the Jap powder monkey when up walked the sergeant, very unhappy because we were loafing.

I proceeded to tell him what an expert our Jap in charge was at shooting off the dynamite, and that not just anyone could do the job. He became very loud and boisterous and said, "If it's o.k. with your boss, I'll come around after work and light the fuses for you."

We spent the rest of the afternoon convincing our Jap he should let the Sergeant shoot off the charges that evening. After he finally agreed, we even got him to shorten the fuses on the charges a few inches. At last the time came. Over came the sergeant displaying his confidence and cockiness to the utmost. He even kept all the guards and prisoners on the job to watch him shoot down the rock.

Ordinarily I'd have taken cover a long way from the rock facing when it was shot down, but tonight I wanted to be where I could see. I got behind a large tree at the side of the quarry. With me was the Jap powder monkey. The Jap Sergeant lit a cigarette to light the fuses with, as was their custom, and confidently strode up to the rock facing. But instead of climbing to the top and lighting the eight fuses on the way down, he started as the bottom and worked his way up. He was about half-way down when she blew. He went sailing out through the air with the broken rock. I guess he never knew what hit him. When the smoke and dust cleared, he was just a crumpled mass, practically covered with stone, about thirty feet from the base of the cliff.

The Jap beside me made a sucking sound through his buck teeth and said, "Jo-to-Nye!" which meant no good.

I thought to myself, "Well, there's another good Jap."

Nothing much was said about his death but the other Japs laughed and made fun of him for being so stupid and getting killed. I remembered stepping out rather briskly as we were being marched back to camp. The stupor-like deadness seemed to disappear from the whole group. There was even singing and laughter to be heard.

My rejoicing over the Sergeant was short-lived when they called for the drilling detail again that night. I immediately broke out in a cold sweat, and visualized getting shot and worse. Instead they marched us back to the rock pile to dispose of the dead Jap. It seemed he was something special back in Japan, and they had us help cremate him. We built a roaring hot fire in a sunken place in the ground, dragged the dead Jap to it and tossed him on top of it. The stink and smell was horrible. I got the dry heaves and thought I was going to die right there.

It took almost all night to finish the job. When the fire had died down the next morning, the Jap in charge scooped up about one handful of ashes and placed them in a cloth in the bottom of a box. This handful of ashes, along with his sword, was to be shipped back to Japan.

On the way back to camp we ran into torrents of rain. I thanked God; it helped wash off the smoke and smell.

The following day I made sick call and bludgeoned my way into the hospital. My buddy Tony was already there, so we immediately set up house for a little poker game. We put up a partition between us and the other sick people in the corner of the hospital, and we were in business. By the third night of the game, the camp monies had ended up, as usual, in the possession of the same old crowd, and the game had gotten down to where there were only four of us bucking heads: Tony, Buck, Nitch and myself.

What a spectacle we must have made, squatting and lying around that blanket, with a small bottle of petrol stolen from the Japs' truck sitting on each corner to provide the light for us to see by.

Tony was dealing five card stud. Buck caught a king, Nitch a queen, I caught a seven, and Tony a ten.

Buck said, "Ill just bet twenty rupies, ten on each king."

Nitch said, "Being you're so generous, I'll just raise another ten on each of my queens."

I dropped out and Tony said, "Me too." Buck called the raise and re-raised the bet; Nitch called and raised again, Buck called and Tony dealt the next card. Buck caught a king and Nitch another queen.

"I'll just bet," said Buck, "after all Nitch, I'm looking down your throat. I got three kings."

Nitch said, "I'm just going to raise and see if you got three of a kind." Buck had to call but waited until the last card was dealt before he raised Nitch.

"Now Nitch," he said, "you see I got three kings showing, so that makes me four. If you can beat them, bet."

Nitch rubbed his long wavy black beard and smiled at Buck, "I just don't believe you got that king in the hole, and I got four queens, so I'll just bet."

"O.K.," said Buck, "how much you got there, just throw it in the pot. I'll cover it." Nitch did, and Buck turned up the fourth king.

Nitch turned white, grabbed the blanket and jumped up. Gasoline and flames flew all over our corner of the hospital. The place lit up like a Christmas tree. Without the help of the rain on the dry roof, we'd probably have had about two hundred sick men burn up. We wouldn't have been able to get them out. As it was, it took all of us who were able to fight the fire about thirty minutes to bring it under control.

Things had just got calmed down when I felt someone shaking me. It was "Copp", our corpsman who said, "Go down to the other end of the hospital and quiet those sick guys down. They are having hallucinations again."

I got up and walked to the other end of the building to the fire in the middle of the aisle. Everyone was quiet but one patient. He was very sick and looked real wild-eyed. He was seeing snakes and kept telling me to get them down, "You're O.K., fellow. Just take it easy, we don't want to disturb all these other guys, do we?"

In a few more minutes we had six or eight guys awake, all seeing snakes. This was a normal reaction for patients with malaria. Someone gripped me by the shoulder. It was Copp.

"Look," he said.

I looked up and froze with horror. There it lay, about six feet above our heads, on the bamboo rafter over the fire. We immediately moved the sick men out from under it, and sent for the guards and their rifles. When they arrived at the door, they took one look at the huge snake and re-treated saying, "Get Butcher Jones and Itch to come and kill it with the ax."

Jones and Itch came running with the ax and a shovel. Jones reached up with the sharp edge of the ax and hook-ed the snake behind the head. He jerked it to the ground and Itch severed it in two with the shovel. It thrashed only once and then lay still. It was a Rock Python that measured about twelve or fourteen feet in length. Evidently it had been driven from the hills down into the camp by the rain and water. It must have come through the roof from a large fig tree alongside, to absorb the warmth of our fire. Anyway, our sick people had snake soup with their rice the next day.

That evening I was sitting on a stump in front of the hospital when up walked a little old dried up Australian.

"Hey cobber," he said, "where's that yank Copp? I got an awful misery in me tooth and they tell me he can pull it for me."

I called Copp and he came out with his old rusty forceps and a sadistic grin on his face.

"O.K., Nick, give him the chair, I'll pull his tooth."

I got up from the stump and let the Aussie sit down and Copp went to work.

"Which tooth is it?" asked Copp.

"Oh, that one," said the Aussie, pointing to a molar in the back of his mouth.

As I held the back of his head, I heard a slight grating as Copp took hold of the tooth with the forceps, and saw only a slight movement of his wrist as he came out with the tooth.

"There you are Aussie, if you have any more, come back. I'll be glad to pull them for you."

"You mean it's out that easy?" said the Aussie as he raised from the stump.

"Yeah," said Copp, "nothing to it."

The Aussie spat, shook his head and turned to walk away. Suddenly he turned around and came back.

"Hey Cobber, while you're at it, and as long as it's that easy, I think I'll just let you pull the rest of these lowers.

Then if I ever get out of this show, all I'll have to do is get my plate made."

Copp pulled the remainder of his lower teeth with ease. Too easy, I thought, so I asked him about it.

"Well," he said, "it really is easy, under these conditions. Lack of vitamins is causing all our gums to recede and our teeth to get loose."

Thinking the situation over that night, I made the decision to get out of the hospital. I was not going to just lay there and deteriorate like all the others.

THE DEATH RAILWAY AT TAM CHANEE. THAILAND.

17

"Another Good Jap"

A couple of days later I found myself again sloshing through the mud and with about forty or fifty other people who had volunteered for an advance crew. We proceeded on into the jungle about twenty-five miles ahead of the large work camps. Our job was to fell all the large trees that would be in the way of the railway.

Tools that were provided for us were very inadequate. I remember one particular teakwood tree that four of us sawed and chopped on for six days before we could get it to fall. Then one morning it seemed to lose its defiance of us and just toppled over. It fell straight down the right of way, bounced and split open like a ripe watermelon. It must have been about sixty or seventy feet high and about nine feet thick at the base. Lovely straight-grained teak, almost enough to deck a battleship. I could practically see the dollars and cents roll up in the smoke as the Japs poured on the gasoline and set it afire. Without any heavy equipment I guess they thought that was the only way we could move it.

For the next three or four weeks I worked for Jap Sergeant, building a small bridge. He treated us quite well, and would give us plenty of time off when we finished his assigned quota of work for the day. When we had finished with driving the pilings and laying the sleepers, our job on the bridge was completed.

For about three days, all we did was march out to work, lay around in the shade, take a bath in the stream, and play cards. It was on just such an afternoon that General Nickatoma and his inspection staff came through checking the railroad. They slipped up on us, and before we knew what was happening, they had our Jap Sergeant before them at attention. When he explained to them that we had worked so hard and finished the bridge ahead of schedule, they seemed very happy and proud of him, but when they checked their blueprints, they found that we had built it thirty-five degrees out of line with where the railroad was to run.

A staff officer screamed, and the Sergeant immediately jumped to a strict attention before him. The beating he received was almost as severe as any I ever saw any prisoner receive. As hardened as I was to this sort of thing, I cringed with each resounding blow he received. I guess it was partly because I knew when the inspection party left, he and the guards would work us over in turn.

However, that wasn't what happened at all. When General Nickatoma and his party left, the Sergeant slowly dragged himself to his feet and staggered over toward us. Holding his battered face between both hands he said,

"Cho-co Joe-toe-Nye." Which meant, "Officer no damn good!"

I knew we'd have to rebuild the bridge, and as I tossed and turned in my sleep that night, I prayed they wouldn't drive us beyond the limit of our capabilities. Early the next morning as the sun began to loom up over the mountains, we already had our rice rations and were standing in ranks waiting for the sergeant to go to work.

We waited and waited, but he didn't show up. Our guards began to get a little impatient, and the corporal called me out and said, "Socho Moch-e-goy." He pointed to the Sergeant's quarters up the side of the hill, and motioned for me to go after him. I started up the path, but when I broke into the clearing, there he lay. I guess he couldn't stand the thought of losing face with his superior officers so he had shot himself during the night. I noticed the blow flies around the small hole under his chin and the swarm of jungle gnats around his one bare foot.

I ran back to the guards and motioned for them to come up the hill. The corporal came running and stood aghast as he viewed the corpse. All he could seem to say was, "Naun-Ne." Silently he turned and motioned me back down the hill. I preceeded him down the hill and fell back in ranks with the other prisoners. That old proverbial phrase once again began to float through the ranks: "Well, there's another good Jap."

They kept us standing there in the pouring rain while each guard in turn gave a glowing lecture on what an honor it was to die for the Emperor. Finally they told us to get packed. We were going back to our regular work camp.

Arriving back at Camp No. 100 after an all-day hike

through the mud, I discovered that conditions were no better than when I had left. In fact, they were much worse. Everyone seemed to have an illness of some kind, and men were dying off like flies.

Our three camp doctors were striving around the clock to save lives. What frustrations they must have suffered when they could see it was an utterly hopeless task they were up against, without medical supplies or even food to feed their patients.

It was about this period of time that my very dear friend and companion, Donnis, came to me seriously ill from being driven to work every day whether he was sick or not. He was suffering from beri-beri, malaria, cholera, and dysentery, and looked like he was on his last legs. I took him to sick call the next morning and made sure he got into the hospital.

Donnis was too good for his own good, and I knew if I didn't speak up for him, he wouldn't say anything in his behalf. I didn't blame the Japs for his condition as much as I blamed the officer in charge of his work detail. He was that no good so-and-so, J.B., who had already killed a number of his own men by forcing them to go to work every day whether they were able or not. By always having the most men in his work detail he made himself look good in the eyes of the Japs.

I slept along side Donnis that night in the hospital to make sure he'd get help if he needed it. All night long he had me awake with his nightmares and hallucinations from his fever. The next morning he was worse and his temperature got up terrifically high. Tony came over to see us, and I asked him to bring me some water to bathe Donnis with.

I proceeded to tear the end from an old towel to use as a wash cloth and brought a small piece of soap to wash him with. By this time Tony had returned with a bucket of warm water. I climbed up on the bunk alongside Donnis and started washing him.

During the time of his bath, I kept up an incessant line of chatter, joking with him to try and cheer him a little. I'd just finished washing him and was giving him a brisk rub with an old towel when I asked:

"How do you feel now?"

"Oh much better," he whispered, "I'll never be able to thank you guys enough."

"Nick," he said, and I leaned down to hear him better.

"Tell Mother," and the words trailed away as he gasped and drew his last breath.

I called the doctor back to check him and make sure, and as he completed his examination he turned to me and said, "Sorry Nick, but I know that won't console you much at a time like this. It's just a shame we have to tolerate officers like that no good S.O.B." He must have seen the bloodlust and hatred in my eyes, because he said, "Now don't you go do anything foolish." I vowed then and there before God and everyone that I'd kill him if it was the last thing I ever did.

We buried Donnis that afternoon, and that night I made my first attempt to get J.B. I borrowed a razor from one of our barbers, who wished me luck. I put it under my pillow and went to bed as usual, thinking that no one had any idea of my plan. About midnight I got out of my bunk and began making my way to J.B.'s hut. I had the razor opened and folded back over my hand so I'd only have to make a swing across his throat. I got to his bunk and raised up the mosquito netting. His breathing was heavy and labored, but it seemed as if my pounding heart was making more noise than his breathing.

Flash! I saw stars, and that was the last I remembered until I came to in my bunk. As I looked up, I slowly began to see Bull sitting alongside me.

"What's the matter with you? You damned fool, you want to get shot, or court martialed and sent to prison for life if we ever get out of here alive? Stop worrying about that no good S.O.B. You know the good Lord takes care of people like that, and he'll get his."

I felt an awful knot on my head and said, "My gosh, Bull, what'd you hit me with? How'd you get me back here?"

He grunted and said, "Shut up and go to sleep or next time you'll get out of these messes by your ownself."

In my prayers that night I thanked God for fellows like Bull who seemed so stable and in control of their faculties at all times.

After a couple of days, I was moved on down the line to Camp No. 115. It was no different than any of the others, maybe worse in some respects. Down the middle of the camp was a low bamboo fence separating us from about five thousand disease-ridden, starving natives.

I was assigned to a Jap crew to help clear space for the railroad ahead of the digging crews. Everything went fine for a few days, until I heard the meow of a couple baby kittens.

Tony was standing alongside me, and we both stopped pulling at the pile of dead brush at the same time. I leaned over to look at the area where the sound was coming from and there they were. Baby jaguars, beautiful yellow with jet black spots. As we reached in after them, they bared claws about one inch in length.

"Hold it," I told Tony, "get me a glove."

He went after a glove and I borrowed an old tropic sun helmet. When he returned, I put the glove on, reached in, and lifted the baby jaguars into the hat. It was about quitting time on the job, and when the guards herded us all together again, one came over and wanted to see what I had in the hat.

"Oh Ossoka," he said as he reached into the hat. He let out a yelp as he jerked out his clawed hand. The other Japs laughed and made fun of him as he stomped in anger. But the Jap in charge asked me if I'd carry them back to camp and give him one. I told him sure, he could have both of them as far as I was concerned. When we completed our five mile trek to camp and the Jap guard came over for his kittens, I was glad to get rid of them.

Strutting up to the front of the officer in charge of the camp, he stood with the hat between his hands as the sentry on duty called the officer in charge. The C.O. came out and acted like a child with a new toy. As yet none of us knew what kind of animals they really were, so they called over a native interpreter. He took one look in the hat and started jabbering and screaming to the other natives. All of them in turn seemed to go berserk. They stampeded the low fences around their part of the camp and fled in all directions.

By grabbing the interpreter and holding him until he calmed down a little, we finally found out what was wrong. His explanation was that as soon as it was dark the mother of the baby jaguars would come back from the hills looking for her young, and since they were gone, she would track them to the camp and kill us all in our bunks.

The Japs began to jabber and point down the road in the direction from whence we'd come, and I could see it coming. We were going to take the jaguars back where they were found. They grabbed off four of us to go back with six guards, and you could sense the feelings of fear as we made our way back to where we had been working all day. As I placed the kittens back in the lair, I looked up and saw some of our guards cutting armloads of branches. Knowing them as I did I figured they were going to work me over. However, that wasn't the case at all. Instead, we walked backwards to camp, brushing out all our tracks as we went. Arriving back at the entrance of camp, we were met at the guardhouse by the officer in charge of the camp standing by a spray gun with two little sickly-looking Jap medics.

They sprayed us all down from head to foot with a disinfectant that smelled like pure creosote. Try as I might, I couldn't scrub off the strong odor. In spite of these efforts to cover our trail, I jumped with fear at every little sound all night long. The disinfectant kept the jaguars away, but the after effects were worse than the spraying. The next morning, our skin was cracked and swollen around our eyelids, and by evening, we had begun to peel.

18

Bridge Work

A couple of days later, I found myself on a pile driving crew for a large bridge. As with every other technical process, the Japs had a very crude but efficient method of driving pilings into the ground. Across the stream they had a large bamboo tower built about sixty feet in height, atop of which were two large pulleys, one on each side. A rope ran through each of these and down the railroad bed about fifty yards in each direction. The Japs would put about a hundred prisoners on each end of the rope to pull the weight up the center rod, then let it fall dead center on top of the pilings, driving them into the shale and muck.

Rather than pull on the weight all day, I volunteered to climb the tower with a little old dumb looking Jap and help hold the driving rod straight. It was really a very simple job, although it was rather dangerous. The top of the tower was about three and one-half feet square. Split bamboo was lashed across two opposite corners to make platforms to sit on. A short rope was looped around the three inch driving rod and the Jap and I each held an end.

After a few hours, the job began to get monotonous. It was now raining just enough to be irritating. The platform had become slick with mud. I looked at the Jap. He was hanging off his platform, supported mostly by the rope.

"Well," I thought, "I know I'm going to let him loose; what am I waiting for? Look at the gleam in the eyes of that sea of faces below. I can't let them down."

"Gotta make it look good so these yellow so-and-so's will think we're both falling."

I waited for tension on the line, and as soon as I felt it, I let him go and grabbed desperately for the center rod as if I were falling myself. Over he went, heels over head. I caught a glimpse of the shiny hobnails on his boots as the sun and rain glistened on them. A few feet down he crashed into the bamboo cross braces, slammed back into the piling, bounced back through the side of the tower and landed about fifteen feet down the creek with a dull thud.

He just lay there on his back in what looked like a broken heap. Our guards all laughed and pointed at him and called him a stupid fool. One of them walked down, kicked him in the ribs, then dipped his tin hat in the water and threw it in his face. The Jap slowly raised his arm, wiped his face off, turned over on his stomach and began to pull himself to his feet. I stared in disbelief. I was sure he was dead. He couldn't have been hurt very badly because he laughed and pointed to the top of the tower. I watched as he walked under his own power out to the road through the jungle, and caught a ride back to camp.

Work the rest of the afternoon was just a farce. Remarks about the animal-like characteristics of the Japs kept up in a steady stream. I remember remarking, "Yeah, I guess if you held one up by the tail and dropped him, he'd land on his feet."

We finally got a break and retreated to a clearing in the jungle for a rest. I was lying in the shade alongside an Australian when a large centipede dropped on his arm.

"Lie still, Aussie. I'll get a banana leaf for him to crawl on." I broke and ran toward some banana trees on the other edge of the clearing, but he couldn't wait until I returned. I heard him say, "I'll knock the bloody bloke off!" He did, but by the time we got back to camp that night, his arm looked as if he had just had surgical stitches removed all down his forearm. Where ever the centipede had crawled, it had injected poison.

A couple of days later, these spots had all ulcerated and the doctors amputated his arm in an attempt to save his life. Their efforts were all in vain; he died from the shock of the operation.

When he lost the Aussie, Dr. Eppi broke down and cried. Then, regaining his composure he said, "If just one of these past twenty-six men who died of amputations would have lived, we could have saved a lot of them. More than anything else, they need faith and hope, plus the will to live."

Poor old Doc's prayers were answered just a few days later, I guess. A Dutch doctor we had in camp brewed up a batch of rotgut whiskey from sweet potato peelings and rice. Before they tried the next amputation, they poured their patient full of it until he was limp with intoxication.

He survived the operation, and it wasn't long until we had quite a number of amputees around camp on make shift crutches and artificial limbs.

Early one particular morning they lined all the American prisoners up and beat us around a little. After an hour or two we finally found out the reason was that American planes had raided their homeland.

After they finished bashing us around, they picked the eighty most healthy looking of us and told us to get ready, we were going to move in the next thirty minutes. That afternoon, during a rest period on the road, they told us we were returning to Camp No. 74 to form a new railhead. Arriving at our destination about dark, we were marched up a hill through the jungle to our new camp. The incessant rain was still beating a tattoo on our backs, and the natives didn't even have our barracks roof on. Whitey and I flopped alongside a tree and stretched a small piece of tarp over our heads.

I had no sooner stretched out than the guards were screaming for us to fall in ranks. A girlish looking little Jap corporal came out and said, "I'm in charge of this camp now. I'm so sorry, but we must go to work now."

"That's great, just great," I remarked, as Whitey and I walked down the hill toward the railroad yard to go to work. "We haven't had anything to eat all day, now they'll probably work us all night without anything." I never realized what a grotesque understatement that was. Two nights later we were still staggering along carrying railroad ties and stacking them under the camouflage of the jungle. People were just dropping from sheer exhaustion and were receiving severe beatings to drive us to continue working.

About midnight I heard the welcome shout, "Chow down, come and get it!" As I climbed down from the box car where I was helping unload ties, I was almost trampled by the hunger-crazed men rushing by. Joining the mad rush, I ran to the chow line. As I moved closer to the food barrel the aroma smelled so good I could hardly wait for my rations.

I could hear Itch, our cook, say, "O.K., take it easy you hodios, we haven't got much for you anyway, just a little nourishment to tide you over until the rice cooks. It should be done in another hour or so, so calm down. You're not going to starve."

With trembling hands I held my battered mess kit over the half-barrel as Itch poured a small ladle into it. Immediately squatted down and started to sip the fluid very slowly, so as to make it last as long as possible. Immediately I realized what I had was hot canned milk. It was so hot and so good, it seemed like a life-giving blood, as I felt its warmth on my insides. As long as I live I guess, I'll always remember the value of that small tin ladle of hot milk and what it did for me. And just think, the average person back home wouldn't even feed it to his dog or cat.

We had completed our third night's work before our relief got there to take over the work so we could knock off and get some sleep. I hardly recognized my former shipmates as they climbed down from the train, which had entered the yard from the opposite direction from which we had been working on the railroad. I was so tired I could hardly keep my eyes open, and had the blind staggers.

Whitey helped me up the mud-slick hill going back to camp, and to our surprise our huts were completed and our galley was built. After stuffing myself until I was bloated on rice, I rolled out my mats and bedding and sacked out. It was the next afternoon before I was awakened by the smell of something cooking. I arose stiff and sore from lying on the split bamboo, and as I slid out of the side of the hut, here was Whitey cooking up a pan of fried rice. While I was eating with him, the Corporal in charge strolled through and told us we still had another day or two of rest coming, so for us to take it easy.

Our freedom here was not quite so restricted because they didn't have fences up yet, and we could go down through the yards to a creek for bathing. Returning from such a bath, Whitey and I walked brazenly up to a Jap supply sergeant and said, "O.K., where do you want this stuff?" While I talked to him, Whitey jerked a bag from the doorway of the boxcar he was guarding, raised it to his shoulder and started up toward camp.

I proceeded to tell the Jap what a no good so-and-so the Jap officer in charge of our camp was for sending us down here after a heavy bag when we were supposed to be resting. He turned to look for Whitey and I ducked under the train to catch up with him.

We stopped on the side of the hill leading up to our hut to take a rest. "What is it?" I said to Whitey. "Sugar?"

No, much better than that," he said. "Salt."

"My gosh, it's worth a small fortune if we sell it by the cupful, five to fifteen rupees a cup, a hundred kilos, that's two hundred and twenty pounds."

"I got a better idea," he said. "Let's ditch it outside of camp where we can watch it and try to sell the whole bag to the other camp."

"Good idea," I said. "Let's put it over there by the stump where I can watch it from inside camp and you slip out the back way and go see if you can make a deal."

Our neighboring camp was separated from us by a bamboo fence, but by going back through the jungle and circling around, we could slip inside their camp without detection. Once inside we were alright, because ordinarily the Japs couldn't tell one prisoner from another.

Whitey left, and I sat down on a stump to guard our sack of salt. I waited and waited for Whitey to return, and I began to get worried about him. So I stopped the first prisoner to come by.

"Hey, mate, you want to make a fast twenty rupees in about five minutes?"

"Sure," he said, "what do I have to do?"

"I'll tell you, see that sack out there by that stump about half covered with grass and brush? You just keep an eye on it until I get back here and see no one bothers it, and I'll give you twenty bucks."

I left him to guard the salt and took off to check on Whitey. I'd only gone a short distance through the jungle when I met him coming back.

"My gosh, Whitey, where you been? I thought maybe the guards caught you or something."

"Naw," he said, "I been dickering with that Dutch officer, trying to get two thousand rupees for our salt; but the most I could raise was twelve hundred. I still think that's better than trying to peddle it by the cupful."

We slipped back into camp and I went out to check our salt. Everything seemed in order, so I paid my watchman his twenty, and Whitey and I went to make our delivery. I got hold of one end and Whitey took the other.

"O.K., heave," I said. We lifted and the bag flew up in the air. Someone had stolen its contents from us and stuffed it full of grass. Not only were we out of a bag of salt, but the twenty rupees also.

We shook the sack out on a blanket and scrounged a couple of cups of salt, but we never could figure out how anyone could pull such a fast switch on us. That night, while working the night shift, Whitey and I slipped back up to camp and searched through everyone's belongings, but it was all to no avail. There was no sign of any salt.

19

Dynamite Fishing

The next day about noon, we were routed out again and marched down into the yards. A train had arrived, and blocked up on two flat cars was a large steel water tank. The Japs made it very clear to us that we were to unload it and place it on top of some large pilings back in the edge of the jungle.

We worked and pried and pushed, but our progress was so slow that after three days we had only managed to tilt the tank over so that the top edge rested against a bank. The bottom still rested on the train cars.

Early on the fourth day, the Japs brought in a trainload of coolies, and what a spectacle that was. They were swarming all over the train, engine and all. They called the coolie boss and explained to him what they wanted done. He just grinned and shook his head and started the coolies to work.

First they went to the camouflaged piles of cross ties in the jungle and carried them over to the track. Using them, they built a wide set of steps to the top of the pilings where the tank was to be placed. By this time they squatted down, unrolled their banana leaves of rice and had their tea. I zealously watched as they palmed their opium, smoked it and prepared their betelnut for chewing.

After a short rest, they all swarmed to the tank. Men, women, children, even babies, on one hip of their mothers, or tied to their backs, almost hid the tank from view like crawling ants. Such an unreal seething mass of humanity I'd never seen before. Even under the bottom they were crowded together, with hands upraised to lift, and where there wasn't room for someone, they'd just reach through with one finger.

A rhythmical chant started to gain cadence and echo off the steel tank down the valley. Gradually the tank began to right itself and slowly move across the tracks. We all stared in astonishment as they carried the tank non-stop through the yards, into the jungle clearing and up the steps, and gingerly placed it on top of the pilings. As each coolie came down he brought a cross tie with him and re-stacked them in the camouflaged stacks in the jungle. By early afternoon their job was completed, so they unconcernedly climbed back on the train and left.

After about a month they finally told us we'd have a couple of days off to do our laundry and camp duties. Bright and early on the appointed morning the corporal in charge of our group called for three volunteers who were good swimmers. Being on his black list, Whitey and I decided to go, thinking we might get back in his good graces, or stumble into something worthwhile. We left the camp by truck, and our next stop was at General Nickatoma's headquarters. Here we were joined by some more guards, and a powder monkey we had met before. We went through the back of the General's camp and headed straight east. After an arduous four or five hour trip in the jungle, we came to what seemed to be a solid wall of horse-like looking weeds. At first I thought the Japs were going to hack a trail through the weeds, but I guess they gave it up as a lost cause.

Instead, four of them picked up another Jap by the arms and feet to toss him up on top of the weeds. When he landed, he began to thrash about and break over the top of the weeds. In the meantime, two other Japs cut two large bamboo poles, and leaned them up into the broken down tops of the weeds, like a catwalk. It was really tough going for about five hundred yards like this. I remarked to Whitey,

"No one will ever believe we're walking eight to ten feet above the ground on the bent tops of these weeds. It's amazing how they support our weight!"

The weeds gradually thinned out, and as we came down to earth again, the ground was what seemed like solid granite, and sloped down to a large winding river. The water was blue-green and the current very fast. It was here I discovered why they had brought us along. They were going to dynamite the fish and they wanted us to bring them in to shore.

The powder monkey taped the dynamite sticks together in bundles of four. While he and the other prisoner went up the river to throw in the charges, Whitey and I wait-ed with the other Japs to retrieve the fish. They warned us not to dive into the river until all four charges had ex-

ploded. The fourth water spout had erupted when three
Japs, followed by Whitey and me, dove into the river.

"Flash!" the whole world seemed to erupt. I saw yellow
spots in front of my eyes, and when I came to, I was being
rolled on the bottom of the river by the strong current. As
I broke the surface, I gasped for air, and my stomach and
chest felt like I had been beaten with a club. I staggered
to my feet on the rocks. A Jap officer grabbed me around
the waist with his arms and squeezed. It felt like a geyser
of air rushed out of me. Immediately I felt relieved and my
breathing came easy.

Everything happened so fast you couldn't keep up with
it. The shocked fish were being carried downstream, so
we had to dive back in the water and start gathering them.
The first two I caught up with were monstrous things,
about three feet long. I found I couldn't swim with both of
them, so I let one go. We must have gotten about three or
four hundred pounds of fish; we had three large baskets
about half full.

It wasn't until now that I realized one of the Jap swimmers who had dived in ahead of us was missing. That
fifth charge the Jap powder monkey had set off had been
too close to him.

I guess the rest of us were real lucky. My skin was cracked
down the front and what I could see looked like a mass of
black and blue welts. On top of all that, I discovered as
soon as I started helping lift the fish baskets that I had the
runs and was passing blood and mucus.

Whitey was practically dragging me as we carried the
fish back to camp, but I managed to stay on my feet until

we reached the Jap headquarters. After that I guess Whitey must have carried me, for I came to in my bunk so sore I could hardly move.

It was because of this condition that I really got clobbered a couple of days later. I didn't move fast enough to suit a Jap guard, so he slipped up behind me and peeled me with a rifle butt. I fell face forward and he stomped me in the back with his rifle butt and kicked me in the ribs. There was a sickening crunch, and pain shot all through my body. After struggling through the rest of the day, I limped back to camp between Whitey and Hank, dragging my feet, and just collapsed on my bunk.

The next morning I had no feeling in my feet and legs, and seemed to be losing my other senses also. I remember Dr. Eppi telling me, "You'll be O.K., Nick, the only thing wrong with you is rheumatism, probably from this change in weather." I'll always appreciate his telling me that, because if he had told me the truth, that my back was broken, I'd probably have thought there was no hope for me, and just laid down and died. But after about three weeks, Bull and Whitey used a little reverse psychology on me and had me up limping around, and by the end of six weeks I was raising as much Cain as ever.

BRIDGE OVER THE RIVERKWAE IN KANCHANABURI, THAILAND.

20

On to Siam

My next move was to the bridge of the "Eight Hundred", so named because of the twenty-eight hundred prisoners which had been killed there attempting to complete the bridge. It was about six pilings high, and made a curve around a high rock cliff over a deep gorge. In all, I'd say it was a block or so long, and had a deadly, sinister look, as if it were leering at you or hovering over you.

We'd work from daylight until dark repairing and replacing the splintered pilings and sleepers which were damaged by American patrol planes. It seemed they'd never bomb the bridge while it was being repaired, only after it was in good repair and ready for a train to cross.

The Japs brought in a company of combat engineers to help us repair the bridge, but to no avail. During a ceremony in observance of the successful repairs, a plane came down the track. We all ran into the jungle to take cover, but the officer in charge of the engineers stood them all at attention under a tree at the end of the bridge, alongside the railroad bed. He had just begun giving them a flowery lecture when the first bomb landed in the middle of them. Their mangled bodies were strewn over the place. After another run, two sections of the bridge were out, and the plane had dropped leaflets on us.

The leaflets they dropped were about the size of a postcard, with a beautiful gloss finish. On one side was a picture of a well dressed Jap soldier, on the back was the mantle showing the remains of a dead Jap. On the inside was the following message:

"We have now bombed out this bridge nineteen times; rebuild it again and we might let you take a train across it."

I was returned to our base Camp No. 100, where I was again made to realize the savagery of the Japanese Army. I was sitting upon the side of a fill by a railroad crossing when a Jap artillery unit came sloshing down the jungle road through the mud.

They had a rope tied to the front of each gun and gun cart. Through the rope were cross pieces of bamboo that the Japs pulled against, four men to a stick. They didn't walk, they practically ran unless they were in deep mud. An officer rode up and down the edge of the road checking to see that no one was goofing off. When they were, he gave them a vicious slap across the back with the flat side of his sword.

As I was sitting there, one Jap stumbled and fell in front of me. A sergeant came back to him, kicked him in the ribs, jerked him to his feet, and shoved him on down the road. He staggered a few steps more and down he went, face first into the mud and rocks. The sergeant called to the officer, who came back and looked down at him.

"Osah," he said, and motioned to carry on. The sergeant took the Jap's rifle and ammunition belt, threw it onto the next gun cart, and kept going. The sick Jap was simply left behind to lie there and die. Our guards wouldn't let us help him, and they wouldn't help him because he didn't belong to their outfit. Finally, after going by him and holding our noses for four or five days, they did have us stop and cover him up one day.

A few days later I saw the same thing happen to a Jap truck driver whose truck broke down near the spot where I was working. Our guards wouldn't help him either. Of course, after he died they helped us strip him and his truck of everything of any value. The more I saw, the more I wondered how they ever captured anything without any teamwork or cooperation in their own army.

Arriving back at camp that night, I was met by Tony who said, "We better get our gear packed, we'll be moving again tomorrow morning, the rumors have it that we are leaving Burma and going to Siam, someplace near Bangkok."

"That's great," I said, "we can't get out of this jungle too quick to suit me. We better try to buy up some different kinds of money, so when we get there we'll have some that is exchangeable for whatever they use."

"Don't worry," Tony said, "I already have it taken care of. I got rid of all our Rupees, and have quite a variety of monies. But you know, that darn Buck has a bagful of Rupees, but he won't change them."

"Hell no," Buck said as he walked up, "This is the only money that talks here, so it's the only kind I want, at least while I'm still in Burma. I'll worry about Siam when I get there. You guys hold the fort down till I get there. My bunch won't leave until next week."

The next night, as I dozed in the doorway of the jolty train car, those horrible memories of Burma seemed like a bad dream of the distant past. I had the feeling that each camp I passed on the way brought me one step closer to some life other than rotting in this living hell forever. It was really amazing how I could sit here in this jolty car and get such a clear mental picture of all that living hell I had just gone through, and how vividly I could recall all those former prayers I uttered, in complete awareness that the others around me might ridicule me, or not even believe in God.

Vivid as my recollections might be, I began to realize the impossibility of telling others of the things I'd seen here, How could I ever tell anyone how it feels to live in another world; a world in which men are driven through torment, suffering, and ridicule until they no longer act like human beings? No matter what words I used to express myself, they'd never believe me. This is probably one of the very few times in our history that we Americans have been thrust into a situation where one minute we have to lie, cheat, or steal for mere existence, and the next minute find ourselves praying to God for forgiveness. Seeing the lust, greed, and other animal-like characteristics of men subjected to such conditions is enough to make even the strongest of us lose faith in humanity.

I always believed it was God's way of subjecting us to the supreme test, to see if we really deserved to live. And I vowed to always accept what might come as another enriching experience, to maybe help me live a richer and fuller life in the future and appreciate some of the things I had always accepted and taken for granted.

My reflections came to an abrupt halt with the sudden lurching stop of the train. Upon disembarking, I discovered we were at a whistle stop called "Tan Juran Briok", in Siam. As I marched through the town I noticed it was no different than anv of the Asiatic towns I'd seen, maybe just a little more Oriental because of the Chinese influence.

They marched us down to our camp. It was no different from any of the others I'd been in except perhaps a little more crowded, and maybe a little more disease-ridden. There was a drought so we had to march to a nearby river for water. This gave us an opportunity to learn the layout of the place. The Japs would stop by one of the other camps and turn us loose inside for a few hours, not to be good to us, but rather so they could see their friends among the guards of the other camps. We prisoners took advantage of the opportunity to see our old friends and shoot the breeze, too.

It was on just such a trip as this that I witnessed the worst torture I ever saw the Japs inflict on anyone. An

Australian lieutenant had built a radio in a water bottle, and the Japs had caught him listening to it, together with nine other men who bunked near him. They shot the lieutenant's nine bunk mates outright. Then they ran a tube down his neck, force-fed him dry rice and water, and staked him out on his back in the tropic sun. It wasn't long until he started to bloat and swell. His agonizing screams lasted about four days. As I approached this gruesome scene one day while going to get water, I saw a Jap jumping up and down on the lieutenant, now horribly bloated. As I drew alongside, I saw that he was dead, and I thanked God that he wouldn't have to suffer anymore. The stench was so sickening I gagged and almost passed out; and I had thought I could stand anything.

21

Slade

My old buddy, Slade, was in this camp. He probably saved my life by preventing me from taking punishment which at that time I could never have endured considering the condition I was in.

I really didn't think much about it when Slade and I slipped out of camp and broke into a high ranking Jap officer's private railroad car. For some of us it was common practice, but as Slade climbed from the car he carried a blood stained box.

"Come on," he said, "We got to get back to camp quick. I just clobbered a Jap in there."

"What's in the case?" I said. "Coffee?"

"Yeah, but got to hurry."

Our trip back to camp was really uneventful, so we took a couple of tins of coffee out of the case and buried the rest under Slade's bunk. I was sick with dysentery, so I bought my way off the working parties and just loafed around playing poker and racketeering for the next few days.

Toward the end of the week, I came by the guard-house from the river. The guards were beating three guys unmercifully for the coffee Slade and I had stolen. I dashed over to Slade's quarters to tell him what was going on.

"Well now," he said, "we can't let someone else take the beating for something we done, can we?" Getting to his feet he said, "I'll go over and tell the bloody so-and-sos I got their coffee." He raised up the trap door under his bunk, got the coffee, put it in a rice sack and turned to me.

"Now Snowy, there ain't no use of both of us going over there, and besides you're too sick to take a beating like they'll dish out for this."

"I'll admit I'm real scared, but by gosh, I'm going with you anyway. It's no more than right."

"Look Snowy, I'm strong. I can take a beating, so don't be dumb. There's no use anyone else getting hurt if I can convince the Japs I got the coffee by myself."

"Well so long, cobbers," he said, swinging the sack to his shoulder. Don't worry about me; them yellow so-and -sos can't get me down."

I watched as he strode brazenly up to the guard-house and dumped the sack out in front of the Japs. Pointing to himself he said, "I stole your damn coffee, and I'm here to take my punishment. Turn those guys loose."

The Japs dropped their teeth, but they did as he requested. In a few moments a Jap Kimpi truck arrived to take Slade away. Five days later the same truck returned to dump Slade out in front of the guardhouse. They carried him to the hospital, so I went over to see how he was.

No one believed that the japs could ever break Slade, but they sure had. He just lay there, staring into space as if he were dead. Holes in his ears, eyelids, and fingernails bore grim, silent witness to the torture he'd endured. Worse yet, they'd given him the rod treatment. This was administered by placing a hexagonal rod about three inches in diameter behind his knees, and forcing him to kneel. Then a Jap stood on each end of the rod and turned it with his feet, log rolling fashion. With Slade, they'd kept this up until the bones were exposed, leaving him permanently crippled. That was the condition in which I saw Slade for the last time; although I did hear later that his legs had healed and he'd learned to walk with his knees half-bent.

Tony and I again made our next move together, to the hospital camp on the edge of Bangkok, Siam. At least they fed us a little better. Fattening us up for the kill everyone thought.

We managed to exchange some of our American money, so after a few days we were living pretty high on the hog. Another group came in and with them was Buck and his sackful of Rupees. To his despair, about the only thing they were good for was toilet paper, so I immediately nicknamed him the "Rupee King." Like the

old proverbial phrase, "Birds of a feather flock together," Tony and I let him sweat for a couple of
days and then loaned him enough money to get started
back in the rackets.

After a few weeks of loafing everyone began to feel
better, and some even began to regain their sense
of humor. I'd just been talking about this to Dr. Eppi
and went out to find Tony and Buck.

I spotted them sitting toward the end of camp by the
fence playing a game of Acey Ducey. When I walked
up, there were two guards standing there on the other
side of the barbed wire, so I saluted them as I was supposed to. They didn't say anything, just returned the
salute and walked away.

Buck said, "I can't beat the so-and-so. I'm glad you
showed up. Take my place and see if you can beat him."
We traded places and I sat down and got into a hot
game with Tony. The guards came back, on the inside of
the fence this time. They watched us a short while,
they screamed "Attention" at us. Tony and I jumped to
our feet, and they proceeded to give us a long lecture on
what a model prisoner Buck was, because when he
came up he saluted them, but Tony and I just ignored
them and went ahead playing.

When I received the first blow alongside the face, I
looked at Buck. He had an expression of the cat that
just ate the canary. I could tell he thought it was
great that the Japs had mistaken him for me, and that I
was taking his bashing for him. Actually, neither Tony
nor I were seriously hurt, and after it was all over, we
could see the humor in the situation too. Also, we real-

ized that it would have been useless to try to explain to the guards what had happened.

Two days later I thought I was going to be killed by one of our own men. I received a roll of bills from over the fence, from a Chinese woman I'd been making a few shady deals with. It was quite a lot more than I expected, but I didn't say anything, I just pocketed it. It was only a matter of minutes until I received a call from the "Terrible Turk." He was an old barroom brawler from Texas, and had traveled as a sideshow boxer with the carnivals.

Before I could say anything or offer any explanation, he made a vicious swing at my jaw. I ducked, trembling with fear, knowing if he ever hit me in the mouth he probably would knock out all my teeth and maybe break my jaw bones so badly that they would never heal. The next thing I knew, he had my chin in his left hand and drew back with his right to smash me square in the face. I felt myself raising to my toes as his powerful grip tightened on my chin.

At this very moment, Bull hurled himself from the top of his bunk onto Turk's back, and a couple of other guys also jumped him.

"Thank God," I thought, they probably saved me from a blow that could have crippled me, or maybe even cost me my life. After getting Turk calmed down enough to talk to, we finally got the situation straightened out by splitting the money fifty-fifty.

Of course his cut didn't last long, because a couple of days later, Tony, Buck, and I got him into a poker game and fleeced him of it.

Tony and I found a secluded cubicle in camp that housed eight Indians from India. Four of them were Mohammedans and four Hindus. Therefore, when stew was served with meat, four of them wouldn't eat any pork, four no beef, so on those days Tony and I would almost get sick eating their rations. The Japs were feeding them all they wanted, trying to get them to join in with the Jap army.

We also played cards with them until it became such a cheating mess we had to give it up. Because of the language barrier, Tony and I would talk back and forth, but after a few days they were doing the same.

It seemed like the very day we started to feel better and get over our illnesses, they told us to get packed, we were being moved again. That afternoon we marched into the railroad station at Bangkok and were again crowded into the hot filthy boxcars like animals.

22

P-40 & Fat Boy

The trip to the coast was long and arduous. After a day or so, nerves became frayed and fellows fought over any sign of food or water. On the second day we were stopped on a siding near a small stream. A Jap in the car with me tossed a bucket out the car door for someone to fill with water. I was nearest the door, so I jumped down to fill it up. As I did so, a Jap guard on the outside of the train grabbed me, and he and two others proceeded to work me over. It wasn't until I was already bruised up and had a severe cut along my eye that the Japs inside my car intervened and got the guards off of me.

Grasping hands pulled me back into the car as it started to lurch and pull ahead once again. Someone put a rag against the side of my eye to stop the flow of blood. In the distance I could hear Copp's voice.

"Alright, you guys, pass him back here where I can get a look at that eye."

Tender hands shuttled me across the laps of the others until my head rested in Copp's lap.

After looking at my eye he said, "sorry Nick, but I'll have to sew you. Just lay still."

From the inside brim of his hat he took the point from a brass safety pin. For thread he unraveled the end of an old piece of canvas.

"O.K., you guys, hold on to him," he said, "I'm gonna go to work now."

It felt like he was pulling the side of my head off every time he pushed and pulled through my hide, so I started begging him to let up."

"Just take it easy, fellow. I'm about done. Just one more stitch and you'll be O.K."

After what seemed an eternity, he finished and they passed me back over to the door by Whitey and Bull and the fresh air. They made room for me and I went to sleep.

I awoke to the smell of sea air. We were stopping to un-load and embark on a small inter-island steamer. They hurried us aboard and we got under way immediately. I talked to a crewman who told me we'd go around the coast and up the river to the city of Saigon in French Indo-China. We'd arrive there at about daylight tomor-row morning if we didn't run into any trouble.

Finding a place where the breeze would hit, I rooted out room to curl up and sleep until I felt the ship bump the dock. To my surprise we were already in Saigon. As the sun came up I could see what a fabulously big place it was. Miles and miles of docks, big refineries, factories, and northward I could see the city in the distance.

About three hours later they gave us a ration of curried rice and they unloaded us onto the docks.

"Well," I thought, "we'll probably have another twenty-five mile walk to get to camp."

"No," Whitey said, "There's one there, just across the street."

Sure enough, we marched through the docks, into the street and stopped before the gates. It was Sunday, and the prisoners had a day off, so we received a noisy welcome when we marched inside.

Little did we know what we were getting into. It was an English camp, which up until this time had contained only two-hundred and thirty-five men who had been confined here ever since they were captured at the beginning of the war. Out of that small number, there were seventy-nine couples of them shacked up together as husbands and wives. They had a club known as the "Penguin Club" made up totally of queers, both officers and enlisted personnel. They had an elaborate constitution and set of by-laws they followed; about flirting with another's wife, divorces, etc.

It was a great surprise to me when I began to hear these things, because up until now and even after three years' confinement, I actually knew of only one American among us who was this way. Of course, there were always rumors floating around about someone, but we always gave them the benefit of the doubt, unless someone made a pass at us. Then we'd clobber him, and sometimes-especially if he was a Limey-we'd lead him on so we could get him clobbered.

It was a horrible situation, but I remember getting the following explanation about it from a couple who called themselves Mickey and Mary.

"Well after all, why should we worry, when we are so happily united together. We don't care if the war never ends; after all the Japs condone our malpractice and we have agreed to take advantage of it to the fullest. We are real sorry if we offend you Yanks, but that's the way it is."

It was here I first met "P-40". He was a pilot of the planes of the same name in the Phillipines when the war started. He was a small skinny character about my size, with a distinct Texas drawl. I knew from our first meeting that he was sure to be some shady character. Why else would he be here with us, instead of with the people who were captured defending the Phillipines?

Shady character or not, we became close friends and slipped out of camp numerous times together. I guess I really didn't realize the danger of these escapes, because up until now the Japs still only had French Indo-China mandated, and the French pretty well ran things in the City of Saigon.

P-40 really had an elaborate set up arranged for the slipping out of camp. He supplied us with these white tropical shirts and pants. Over these we zipped flight overalls to conceal them until we were away from camp. Then he had a hiding place in which to stash the flight overalls until we returned from the city.

On one such night, we had made contact with a French agent and received a suitcase of medicine for our camp doctors from him. We had replaced the overalls, crawled back through the swamp to our signal post. Here we had a fine wire which ran over the fence into camp. By pulling on it our buddies in camp could signal us by three short jerks, all was clear, that the Japs were at the far end of their patrol area between the two barbed wire fences.

P-40 and I both pulled on the wire, but got no response. We waited but still no answer. P-40 nudged me and motioned for me to crawl ahead to the outside fence.

I crawled to within a couple of yards of the outside wire and cautiously unhooked the strands of wire around the hole where we always went through. This done, I shoved the suitcase through and followed. I thought I was seeing things when I turned to motion P-40 through, all I could see was the legs and rifle butt of a Jap guard. I didn't realize he was standing there leaning on his rifle asleep, so I jumped up, threw the suitcase through the next wire and dove through myself. P-40 clobbered him, but not before he uttered a muffled yell and fired his rifle, bringing all the guards swiftly down upon us.

"My God, give me strength," I prayed as I started sprinting through camp, pursued by the onrushing Japs. It's amazing how fast you can run when your life's in danger, I knew that if I got by the next two huts, I could cut between the cookhouse and the wood shed and lose them in the shadows. Throwing the suitcase under a table as I ran by, I headed for the dark side of the kitchen.

That very day while we were out of the camp, a barbed wire had been stretched between the cookhouse and the work shed. I hit it going full blast. It was only waist high and it flipped me when I hit it. I hung there dazed with the deep barbs of the wire embedded in my thighs. Try as I may, I couldn't get one leg loose from the wire.

Strong hands grabbed me, jerked the wire from my leg, lifted me over the fence and said, "Hod for damma, sew the meter up."

"Thanks," I said, as the warm blood began to flow down my trembling legs. At about the same time the first pursuing Jap also hit the fence and started screaming for help, but his cries were to no avail. Moe, the strong Dutch woodcutter who had pulled me from the fence, just lay in his bunk and ignored him. This gave me the opportunity I needed. During the excitement I milled in with the other prisoners and slipped back to my own barracks.

The next morning I limped over to the back of the galley and met P-40. He asked me if I'd like to try another escape with him sometime soon.

"What? You nuts or something? After all, I don't have to square myself with Uncle Sam like you do."

"Oh, you know." he said. "That being the case, I might as well tell you about it. When the Japs blew up all our planes in the Phillipines and the high-ranking were evacuated, I was left behind as senior flight officer. First they assigned me a company of Gook Scouts, and left us to repel a Jap invasion, which was almost an impossible task without equipment. Oh, yes, I was quite the hero; received the Silver Star and all kinds of awards. After this action I found myself in charge of a motor boat hauling supplies from Manila to Corregidor with two other fellows. It was on one of these trips, when the boat was loaded to the gunnels, that we decided to try to get away and evade the onrushing Japanese and escape sure death or capture. Our passage across the South China Sea took us ten or twelve days, but we finally made it here to French Indo-China. We posed as civilians for a few weeks and really lived it up until we ran low on money, then we were turned over to the Japs. The rest you know about, so you see, I really do have to escape to square myself before the war is over or they might charge me with desertion."

"Yeah, I feel for you, but I can't reach you. Of course, if the opportunity avails itself to where you think we can make it, just count me in. Anything will be better than being starved and worked to death."

I left P-40 and went out to the "tongs" to take a bath. The "tongs" were just a large square concrete tank with an apron around the edge to stand on and soap down. Then we'd dip water out of the tank to rinse off with. There were three or four people there besides myself. One of them was known as "Fat Boy. He was from Georgia and was about five feet two inches tall, but his normal weight was about two-twenty. He was an ex-convict and bootlegger in the States and had the words "Hard Luck" tatooed across his knuckles.

He and I were joking about rum running in the South

when all hell broke loose. Four American "B-25's" slipped in suddenly and started strafing us. I dove into the bath tong and prayed a fifty caliber didn't come inside with me. When the firing ceased and things quieted down again, I climbed out.

"Hey you-all, help me up out of here."

It was Fat Boy. He'd dived into the garbage pit with all the maggots and dysentery refuse from the latrine buckets. The stench was almost unbearable, so I got a stick to pull him out with. As we threw water on him to wash him off, he kept up a constant roar of swearing:

"Any so-and-so that doesn't have any more sense than to dive in this crap should get shot."

About that time the planes made another run and opened up with the fifty caliber machine guns again. The automatic, unthinking nature of people's reactions when their lives are in danger is something I'll never get over. When B-25's had finished their second run, we had to fish Fat Boy out of the latrine again!

23

"Help Nippon"

A few days later I was working at one of the large refineries helping to fill fifty-gallon drums with high octane aviation gasoline. Again the planes slipped in on us and before I knew what happened, they opened fire on us. A B-25 came swooping straight down over the trees at me. When I first looked up I thought it was on fire. Then the lead started plowing up things in front of me. I realized my mistake and took off running down the road toward the guardhouse. A large Australian was running stride for stride with me. Ahead of us, by the fence, two little jap guards were trying to set up a machine gun to keep us in the refinery until after the raid.

"What are you going to do, Aussie!" I screamed.

"Going through the bloody so-and-sos."

I pulled over closer to him and saw that he was carrying a large wrench we used to tighten the caps on the barrels. By this time one of the planes had circled around and was coming down the road behind us, those Jap guns looked mighty small. As we went through the gate, one of the little Japs lunged at me with his rifle and bayonet. I literally threw him aside. As I did so, I heard the crunch of the wrench on the other's skull as the Aussie peeled him.

I sprinted to the first row of trees and dove headlong into them for cover. As I got my breath and bearings, I picked out a large date tree to get behind. Clinging to it like a second bark, I felt something tugging at my pants. Looking down I saw the Little Jap I had knocked out of the way when I came through the gate. Pleadingly he looked up at me and said, "Help Nippon!"

How much like a little baby," I thought, "clinging to my apron strings."

He must have thought he was safe close to me. I couldn't get rid of him. By this time the four planes circled and were getting ready for another run. It looked like they were going to crossfire on the grove where I was. Once again I took off, but I'd just left the edge of the trees when I hit a hole and found myself about shoulder deep in muck and water.

About the time the planes opened fire, I frantically grabbed the little Jap and held him in front of me for protection. I thought to myself, "How foolish can you get? If one of those fifty calibers hit him, it would tear my head off."

As the planes roared on past, I discovered I couldn't get out of the caraboo wallow by myself. I screamed at someone running by, and he stopped long enough to extend a hand for me to pull up on. As I did so, I pushed the little Jap under and stepped on him, but when I reached solid ground here he clung to my ankle and had been pulled up with me also.

After seven runs on the place, the planes left and the Japs sounded the All Clear and started rounding us all up again. It took quite some time, because there were about a hundred and fifty of us scattered in all directions. While we were waiting, the little Jap and I took quite a lot ribbing from the other Japs and prisoners for being so wet and muddy.

By this time the Japs had realized they had a dead guard, so they lined us up on each side of the road for interrogation. Out came the Jap officer in charge to question us. Of course, if there was ever a look of innocence, we all did our best to display it. He begged and pleaded with us to tell him who hit the Jap guard with the wrench and who was the first one to come out the gates.

After a couple of hours and their slappings, all to no avail, he called up the little Jap who had been with me for consultation. He stood him at attention and beat him unmercifully for about fifteen minutes, jerked him to his feet and told him to go down the line and pick out the first two prisoners to approach the gate when the planes came.

My knees trembled with fear, for I knew this was it. He very slowly and deliberately looked everyone over as he came down the line toward me. He now stood in front of me and looked me over from head to foot, but showed no emotions at all as he looked me in the eye and moved on to the next person.

"Surely," I thought, "that officer alongside him can hear my heart pounding and my knees knocking."

Desperate prayers raced through my mind, for I knew if they didn't find the guilty party they'd probably just grab off about ten innocent people and shoot them. I knew I could never let this happen--or could I?

I never did quite understand why the Japs gave up and marched us back to work without carrying out their threats, but they did. Any other time they would have looked for an excuse to bump off a few of us.

Later that night the little Jap came around to see me and thank me for saving his life. He gave me cigarettes, tooth powder and other rations, so I played it up big for him, and bled him dry for the next couple of months.

24

The Tattoo of Death

The nightmare I'd been having dovetailed into the maniacal screaming of the guards. After a quick "Tinko" we were herded into the truck for our usual hectic ride to the Saigon airport. Work here consisted of loading planes, repairing and building runways, and the other usual run of work to help the Japs' war effort.

When I worked here I was never too busy to throw a little sand in the fuel tanks of their planes, or remove the pins from their landing struts. On this particular day I was working with a bunch of Australians, carrying baskets of small stones to patch bombed out holes in a runway. For about two months now we had been getting bombed and strafed continually, so I wasn't surprised when the Japs bent the red flag on the airport tower to signal us to take cover, the planes were on the way.

In the large open area where I was, we were fortunate enough to have an "L" shaped trench to take cover in. I had no more than uttered my usual prayers when all hell broke loose. Sweeping in from my right came about twelve P-38's with their guns blazing as they strafed the airport.

The tattoo of death seemed to echo throughout the vast airport. The guns seemed to literally plow up the runways, striking the Japanese planes parked under their camouflage and igniting them into flames. After seven runs on our area, a sudden hush fell as the planes disappeared.

"Where's the bloody Jap guard?" someone remarked. "He's gone."

"He couldn't be gone" I said, "there's no place to go. But there's his gun."

About this time I heard a faint cry of "Hodio! Mo Chee-goy." Following the call, we discovered that the trench in which we'd taken cover ran in the side of an old, dried up native well. Shading my eyes, I looked down into the round, dry hole, Around the sides dangled the broken pieces of ivy-vines that had concealed the well. Peering up at me from a depth of about twenty feet was the Jap. His leering, evil face had suddenly changed to one of tenderness and mercy as he stretched his hand toward me and pleaded for help.

An Australian alongside me said, "Blimey, what a glorious opportunity. Let's cover the bloody bastard up!"

In utter amazement I said, "You mean bury him alive?"

"Get a shovel. I'll show you what I mean."

I hastily looked around, but discovered we had no tools with us. About two hundred yards away, there was a pile of logs and refuse which we decided to drop in on top of the Jap.

In jubilation I dropped in the first log and heard it hit the Jap with a dull thud. He bawled like a sick calf as the prisoners now in a frenzy, rained debris down on him from above. The well was about half full of logs, tree limbs, etc. before someone called a halt and said,

"We sure better play it cool, and mill back into the larger working parties. It's about time to go back to camp." Before leaving I picked up his rifle and dropped it in on him bayonet first.

I breathed a sigh of relief as I got lost in the crowd of three or four hundred prisoners waiting in front of the tool shed for the trucks to haul us back to camp. Evidently the guard wasn't missed, and nothing was said.

The next morning I was squatted alongside the cookhouse eating my meager ration of rice when an Australian officer walked up and said,

"Snowy, I don't want you or those fourteen men of mine going to work on that airdrome for a couple of weeks more; and don't give me that innocent look. You know what I'm talking about."

In order to stay clear of the airdrome for awhile, I volunteered for a special detail and ended up on the dock handling drums and loading ships. After about three weeks, I began running a little low on the tobacco that I had racketeered for at the airport so I decided to take a chance and return.

There was a spring-like freshness in the air the morning I returned, but as the trucks slammed to a stop, the first thing I saw was the Jap we had buried in the well, sunning himself on a log alongside the tool shed. I practically froze in my tracks, before it dawned on me to hide behind the other fellows to keep him from seeing me.

It was too late. He screamed at me, "Hodio, Mochee-Goy!"

I tried my best to ignore him, but he sent another guard over to bring me to him. As I felt the bayonet nudge me on the butt, a million thoughts raced through my mind.

"Well, this is it, I guess. If they don't kill me outright, I'll never survive the beating I'll get." Standing quietly in front of him, I looked first at his arm in a sling and his bandaged shoulder, then to his bandaged head. Not knowing what to expect, when he smiled at me I got the weak trembles, so great was my relief.

"You my friend," he said. "Sit down." Handing me a cigarette, he joined me on the log and proceeded to give me a glowing account of how I'd saved his life! Using his rifle as a lever, he had taken the junk we'd thrown in the well on top of him and built steps to climb from the well!

As I sat there shocked with disbelief, he expressed in his own way that he was eternally grateful to me and would always be my "Tam-ah-da-shi", or friend. But being ever vigilant to get something for nothing, I was quick to capitalize on the stupidity of my new-found friend. In about three days I had him cleaned out of money, cigarettes, tooth powder, and all his other personal belongings that were of any value to me.

BRIDGE OVER THE RIVER KWAE
KANCHANABURI

25

Milk Runs

The Good Lord sure does funny things. It was just a few days later when I found myself again herded in a jam-packed box car rattling northward up the coast of French Indo-China. On the second day we turned inland, and after about two hours all hell broke loose. The train jolted to a screeching halt. Realizing that the deafening roar I heard was four large four-engine American bombers, I dove from the boxcar into the bank of a railroad cutting and slid down into a ditch.

After four strafing runs on us, our frantic efforts of waving blankets and shirts got the message across. The planes dipped their wings to us and left. Gasping a prayer of thanks, I began to survey the damage around me. I was happy to find all my buddies had escaped without any serious injuries. Two members of the Jap train crew were dead and the bullet riddled engine was beyond making anymore headway, so here we were out in the middle of nowhere without transportation or communication. Our Jap guards were as scared as we, and at a loss for words to tell us what to do.

I looked at the Jap "Sojo" in charge and said, "Yasama."

He said, "Yes, O.K.," and pointed to some bushes on the side of a small hill. Here we took cover again, just in case the planes returned, and lay down to rest while the Japs decided what to do.

Some time later, the Japs awakened us and marched us toward some foothills of the inland mountains in the distance. About dark we reached a small station and railhead at the bottom of a steep mountain. It was the take-off point for cogwheel and cable controlled French trains which climbed into the mountains. It was about a six hour climb to the crest of the summit, after which the track leveled off onto a downgrade, back between the mountains, to the town of Dallot. We were herded aboard these cable cars and began the long climb. The sides of the box cars became very cold and I shivered with the change in climate.

The scenery in the mountains was breath-taking, and the rich fertile valleys seemed to yield enough food even for us who were prisoners. Our work here consisted of digging a maze of tunnels through the granite-like mountains for the Japs to use as storage and headquarters.

Among the oddities of the mountain climate were the clouds that would loom over the top of a mountain and drench us with rainfall numerous times each day. I had only been here long enough to adjust to the climate when I heard the murderous sound, "Hodio! Tinko!" and discovered once again we were going on the march to be moved.

After an uneventful trip back to the coast, I found myself again squashed against the side of the doorway in a jam-packed boxcar heading north along the coastline of French Indo-China. I viewed the long tunnels and bridges with awe-struck disbelief. Little did I know that very soon I'd be praying that they were not my tomb.

For the next three days our train played cat and mouse with the American planes making their daily "milk runs" up and down the railroad, bombing and strafing anything that moved.

We reached the city of Hanoi about daybreak, but without any rest, were marched on north to a native village and our new camp, converted from a native school, surrounded by a bamboo and grass matting fence.

As soon as I saw it, thoughts of escape started racing through my mind. The lack of security and the gaping holes in the fence seemed to spell out an invitation to freedom. Out of a clear sky I was startled back to reality by some inner voice which said, "Take it easy! Don't be dumb! Size up the situation so you don't gamble or take any more chances than you have to."

When afternoon came, the Japs roused us out to go to work on the bridge we had come to repair. It was the same old story; the American planes only bombed the bridge when it was in good repair. As long as it showed signs of not being able to handle trains, they'd just fly over and ignore it.

It was on one such run that our stupid guards opened fire on a modified "B-17" and all hell broke loose. Back he came, guns blazing as he laid a stick of bombs down the tracks and across the bridge near us. As he circled around, I could see his outboard engine on the starboard wing catch fire and go dead. He attempted to turn out to sea, gain altitude, and head to his home base, but his wing tip dipped and hooked the top of a large tree under which we were taking cover. As he boomeranged into the ground, it felt as if the whole earth was erupting. In terror-stricken awe, I saw the tail gunner go sailing out through the air; gun, blister and all. He landed fifty or sixty yards away from the plane, escaping the flames now engulfing the wreckage on the ground.

As the noise of the crash subsided, we became aware of the screams of the wounded trapped inside the plane. One image, engulfed in flames, raced to the water and dived in. At the same time, I saw two prisoners coming toward us, dragging a body that they had pulled from the burning hulk. They'd seen his hands grasping the hatch combing, and had literally jerked him from the inside.

By this time the Japs swarmed in from all sides to capture the helpless plane crew. Their first act was to get them away from us so we couldn't communicate with them. In their usual brutalizing manner, they tied their hands behind their backs and shoved them down the road toward the Kimpy headquarters.

For three days and nights that I know of, they were

prisoners in a hole in the ground by the Jap guard-house, without decent food and without medical aid for the two who were severely burned.

The fourth day after the crash I planned to escape, and that night I slipped through the bamboo matting wall and took off. I ran breathlessly for about an hour or so, until I knew it was safe to relax. Walking back from the beaten path, I found a place to sit down and rest and get my bearings. I knew now that I was only about a mile from the mouth of the river and a native village on the coast. If I could get there, I had hopes of bribing a native out of an outrigger and food. Then I'd head out to sea and wait to be picked up by an American submarine or ship.

As the moon slipped behind a large cumulus cloud, I crept stealthily down to the beach, into the native village, and casually walked up to them.

One turned to me and said, "Hodio!"

I froze in my tracks. My heart pounded. I knew he was a Jap even though he was standing there in only a G string. As the moonlight again crept across the sand and swept over us, I realized he was one of our camp guards and had no business being here either.

Naturally, my first thought was to try and bluff him, so he wouldn't think I was trying to escape.

I said, "Sake-Jo-toe."

He replied, "Toc-Son Joe-toe!"

"Oh," I said. "You're pulling a fast one on the Sergeant, over here having a party when you're supposed to be standing watch."

He let me know real quick-like I was all wrong, and called inside a hut for three of his buddies who came staggering out loaded to the gills on sake and rice wine. They had a drunken discussion on what to do with me until they finished their party. Another Jap staggered out with a bottle in each hand. Thrusting one at me, he said.

"Hodio Sake I-Rue!"

The vile milk-like fluid from the dirty green bottle soon had me on cloud nine. The next time I regained consciousness, I was being kicked to my feet by the guards in front of the guardhouse back at camp. I didn't even know who I was, much less where I was or how I got there.

Regaining my senses, I realized I was being shipped someplace else, "My God," I thought, "Probably to another dingy native prison to be thrown into solitary and die like a trapped rat."

Next I was violently thrown into a truck with three living skeletons. They were the remains of the crew from the airplane crash I had witnessed a few days back. Surely they couldn't live long. They were the most emaciated men I had seen in some time. Not only were two of them severely wounded and burned, but they had that hollow look and ashen gray color you get just before death. I uttered a silent prayer for them and hoped the two Jap guards in the back of the truck with us would be human beings enough to let me try and help them on this trip.

"God," I thought to myself, "It's amazing how you forget your own aches and pains when you see the perils and suffering of someone else in worse shape than you."

I broke into the conversation with the Jap guards, softly at first, and found out from them that they were taking us back to Saigon to the city jail so these three could be interrogated. I knew it was going to be a jolty, arduous trip so I settled down in one corner of the truck bed to make the most of it. Every hour on the war-torn roads seemed like days in the hot sun. After what seemed like weeks instead of days, we finally reached our destination.

They locked me in a cell with the three others and told me to look after them. But how can you help sick and wounded people with nothing to work with?

26

The Escape

I remained confined with the downed airmen for three days. Then, instead of being returned to the main prison camp, I was taken to the base hospital camp and turned over to the doctors. By doing this, I guess the Japs thought they'd make the others think I had been shot. Being in better shape than most of the sick, I went to work for the doctors and also spent part-time as an interpreter for them.

As I stood in the front entrance of the doctor's quarters one morning, a Jap officer came strutting through the front gate with three guards and a white woman. Even though she had been badly beaten, the woman was still nice looking. The Jap officer shoved her toward the doctor and said,

Fix her!"

Doc Eppi took her inside and laid her on a bunk to examine her.

Shaking his head he said, "She is in horrible shape with a fallen womb. There's nothing I can do for her without tools and anesthesia for an operation."

While I talked to her, Doc tried to explain to the Jap officer what was wrong with her and why he couldn't help her.

"So sorry," he said. "She's under contract as a prostitute for the Nippon army, to go to bed with thirty-five soldiers a day. If she can't, she must die."

That's all there was to it-all cut and dried. As they marched her out the gate she said,

"Don't worry about me, I'd rather be dead. You people will never know the suffering and horrors we English girls have gone through."

Slap! She received a belt across the mouth for talking. I watched as they marched across the street with her and stood her against a tree.

"My God," I thought, "surely they are not going to shoot her out on the street in full view of everyone!"

The Jap officer went through the tantalizing formality of removing his sword and giving slow deliberate commands for the execution. The rifles cracked and she slumped to the ground. The Jap officer said something to the three guards. They all turned and climbed into his command car and left.

"Dear God," I prayed, "please let me forget this horrible tragedy, and that look on her face of being so all alone as she stood there frail and quivering before dying."

Someone's hand gripped my shoulder, and a voice

said, "Don't let it bother you, son, she's better off dead."

Looking around I saw it was Doc Eppi with crystal-like tears streaming into his graying beard. I felt sick and weak-kneed as I clung to him and sobbed.

"Go lay down and take a nap son, you'll feel better when you awaken."

Once again I prayed, thanking God for men like Doc Eppi. Surely, I thought, having him to confide in and share mutual feelings with is like having a father to guide me.

That afternoon I was aroused from my slumber by a Dutchman, who had entered the camp as a patient from the main P.O.W. camp down by the docks. He brought me a note from P-40, and in part it said,

"Snowy, glad you're back. How is it in the hopital? Could we get away from there pretty easy? I have con-nections. Will you go? Give me the word. Good luck. P-40."

Two days later I got a message through to P-40, which in part said,

"Everything Jo-to! What are you waiting on? Snowy."

After meeting all incoming patients for about a week, I gave up waiting for P-40 to show and finagled my way to return to camp and go back to work. On the way back we met a group of new sick people, including P-40.

"Well, it's too late now," I thought. But I yelled and waved to P-40 and wished him luck. That was the last time I ever saw him.

For the next few weeks the Allied air raids were astonishing in their precision. I recall in particular one day when a lone dive bomber came swooping in, dropped two bombs, and blew up two large underground fuel tanks. We'd buried them almost a year earlier, and they were well camouflaged, with trees and shrubs growing over them. Everytime something like this happened, it sparked rumors that P-40 was somehow managing to direct the Allied plane crews from the ground. He must have had it at some point, though, because I never heard from him again.

With all the rumors flying hot and heavy, I began once again to contemplate making connections for escape. I thought the smartest thing to do was just keep my mouth shut and my eyes open and see what developed. In a mixed group like this camp, it was so easy to say something to the wrong person. Under these adverse conditions people would slit your throat for something to eat, so you knew they'd turn you in to the Japs to help their own situation, or to get extra food and privileges.

It was with reverence then, that I only listened when I was approached by Gunner McComb and he related his brain storm about escaping to me.

He always reminded me of an old time huckster, trying to peddle his wares, and had thereby received the nickname of Pack-rat. Staying very much alone and ignoring the ridicule of everyone, he seemed happy to live in a shell all his own. Because of this I was rather leery of much association with him. He just didn't seem sharp enough on the trigger to suit me.

Nevertheless, when I slipped out of camp a few nights later, I took Gunner with me, somewhat against my better judgement. My intent was to eat some decent food, meet Frenchy, who was a French racketeer that worked for the Japs, in order to pick up the medical supplies he managed to slip to our camp doctors about once a week, and sneak back into camp before daylight. None of Gunner's escape schemes for me; not yet, anyway.

My first stop, to Gunner's surprise, was at a small Chinese restaurant on the outskirts of Saigon, where I always went to eat and trade for something to drink. I was aghast to see Frenchy come walking nonchalantly through the front door.

"Hi, Frenchy," I said, "You're kinda out of your territory, aren't you?"

"Haven't you heard the latest? The war's about over."

"Somebody never gets the word," I said. "Why doesn't someone tell the Japs. Maybe they'd turn us loose."

"No, really, no kidding. If you don't believe me, you boys come with me, to my house, and you can listen to the radio and hear for yourself. I'm no longer under the strict surveillance of the Japs, so you're welcome to come."

I looked at Gunner, who was half-tight by now. He just shrugged his shoulders, so I knew it was okay with him. Turning to Frenchy, I said,

"O.K., let's go."

We walked silently through the city, circling around

the main thoroughfares until we reached the French residential sector of town. He led us down an alley and through the archway of a stone fence and said,

"This is my home."

It was typical of all the rest of the houses in the area; small, stucco, with red tile roof. I was dazzled by how immaculately well kept the place was.

No sooner was I seated in a large leather chair alongside the radio, than a house boy handed me a cold bottle of French wine. Needless to say, anything cold tasted delicious to me. Before I knew it I was sound asleep or passed out in the chair.

During this time I had very vivid dreams of the Jap officer who just recently sat down beside me on a pile of dirt, took out his sword, put the point under my ribs and said,

"Do you hear any news?"

"No," I said, "only rumors."

"You listen," he said, "the Americans are sinking all our ships, shooting down all our planes, and blowing up our homeland. But that's O.K. After the war's over, they'll all dig down in their pockets and build it back for us."

I awoke saying, "Yeah, we probably will," to see the sun shining in across the floor.

"Oh, no!" I cried, as I leaped from the chair to the window and saw it was daylight.

"What's the matter?" someone said. I turned and saw

Frenchy. Gunner was gone.

"But you don't understand; it's daylight and they've already missed me at camp. They'll shoot me on sight. I'm an escaped prisoner."

He grinned and said, "Have no fear, we will protect you from the Japs."

"We," I said, "who's we?"

"Our underground. It is very well organized here you know. Come with me, I'll have to hide you until arrangements can be made to take care of you."

I followed him out the back door, around the side of the house and into a basement like an air-raid shelter. Here I spent the rest of the day in nervous anticipation of what was ahead of me. Gorging myself on decent food and over indulging in Frenchy's wine, I somehow got through the day.

As dusk came, I was shaken from my stupor by Frenchy.

"Come on." He said, "We have no time to lose. Arrangements have been made. I must take you to the Hotel immediately. Get into this clean shirt and trousers, and if anyone stops us, let me do the talking."

"I must be sick, drunk or dreaming," I said to myself.

"Or maybe I've come down with the fever, again. Whatever it is, I don't think I should be in such a daze, without the power of concentration, knowing what's happening to me, but not being able to do anything about it."

27

Going Home

The incessant drone of the planes caused me to leap to my feet and race to the window. Peering out, my heart raced jubilantly, as between the breaks in the skyline I saw what appeared to be wave after wave of American planes flying over. The explosions were deafeningly near. When the raid finally ended a deathly silence seemed to descend on the whole city.

There was a gentle knock at the door, then a voice,

"Open up, it's me."

Immediately I recognized the voice as Frenchy. I unlocked the door and as he stepped in, he said,

"How are you feeling?"

"Fine," I replied, "how long have I been here?"

"Oh, just a few days, but you must come with me now. The Americans have landed, and I'll see you get to them. You must realize I can no longer protect you, it's too dangerous."

As we rode in the rick-shaw with the blinds drawn, he explained to me that the Americans had dropped paratroopers behind the airport. He was taking me to a drop-off point from which I would be able to reach American lines.

"Frenchy," I said, "I don't even know your name, but I want you to know I sure appreciate what you have done for me the last few days. God only knows what would have happened to me if it hadn't been for you."

"Ah, 'tis nothing," he said, as he extended his hand to me in warm friendship. "But I'm sorry, I must leave you at the next corner. Goodbye and good luck. Someday we'll meet again."

I left the crossroad and took cover toward the airdrome in the bushes to size up the situation. Sure enough, Frenchy was correct; in the distance out on the airfield I could see the Americans in their shallow trenches.

"I'd better play this safe," I thought. "I'll take off my clothes so they will at least know I'm a white person and on their side. Among the crackle of small fire arms, I raced madly across the field on their flank hysterically screaming, "Don't shoot! Don't shoot!"

I jumped into the trench and froze. The cold barrel of a machine gun was pushing in my guts. All I could see was the cold eyes of the tall French Canadian holding the gun.

A little Major grabbed his arm and screamed, "Hold it!"

Looking at me he said, "Who are you?"

"I don't know," I stammered, "but you speak my language."

With this, I cried and sobbed with joy, and slumped to the bottom of their trench.

The tall fellow yanked me back to my feet and said, "Don't just lay there, take this gun and start shooting!"

"But I don't know how to operate that kind. The tommy gun I was trained on had a pan of shells, instead of this clip."

"Don't worry about it. I'll fix it. You just pull the trigger."

This was my introduction to the O.S.S. I thanked God for my luck, because I found out real quick that they shoot first and then ask questions.

There were only a handful of them left, but another waves of planes came and more bailed out. It wasn't long until the Japs only offered passive resistance, and they took the airdrome.

Two days later they moved into a hotel downtown for their headquarters. I guess the war was all over but the shouting, and I didn't know it until fourteen days and as many skirmishes later.

I became an interpreter for the O.S.S. because I had a little knowledge of "Nippon Go", the Jap Army language. Without any doubt I got my revenge for all the tortures and punishments I had received in the last three and one-half years.

The morning of the fifteenth day I found myself an old salt with the O.S.S., and jostling along in a jeep with the Major, Frenchy and a driver headed for the airdrome. We parked about sixty yards from the runway and waited for the combat cargo planes to bring in our supplies and more equipment. A lone C-46 circled the airport and made a glide down the runway, kicking out supplies through its side hatch.

Meantime the little Major was talking to them with his ground to plane communication.

"Snowy," he said, "the next time that plane comes down the runway, I want you out there."

"What for?", I said, "There's snipers shooting out there. It ain't safe."

"That doesn't make any difference, I want you out there to get on that plane. I have orders to send you home."

Unbelievable as it was, I bade my farewells, said "Thanks," and jubilantly sprinted to the edge of the runway, as the plane started in.

It didn't come to a complete stop, and as I battled the prop wash to get alongside, it seemed like it would take me forever to get to the hatch. Two characters on the inside leaned out, grabbed my wrist, jerked me inside, and we were on our way.

I was amazed at the plane and crew. Instead of all the spit and polish I'd always associated with the Air Force, the two characters standing beside me had beards, filthy dirty clothes, and looked like a couple of tramps. There were no seats in the plane, most of the windows were broken, there was horse dung on the deck, and back on the starboard side there was a hole big enough to jump through.

"My God," I thought, "if these are the kind of guys who've been winning the war, I'd have been better off to have stayed with the Japs."

A gentle nudge on my arm, and a broad grin on one of the crew's face immediately changed my thoughts, as he led me forward in the plane.

The radioman reached out and pulled me into his shack and placed a pair of earphones on my head.

"Here, listen to this."

It was music, heavenly music, and large tears streamed down my face as I heard them sing, "Going Home!"

"Thank God!" I said, "Maybe I'll never have to hear that word "HODIO" again!"